Catholic Mental Health Ministry:

Guidelines for Implementation

Catholic Mental Health Ministry: Guidelines for Implementation

ISBN: 978-0-578-22536-4

Printed in USA by 48HrBooks (www.48HrBooks.com)

CATHOLIC MENTAL HEALTH MINISTRY:

GUIDELINES FOR IMPLEMENTATION

Wendell J. Callahan, PhD
Executive Director & Professor of Practice

Liberty Hebron, MA, LPCC
Mental Health Ministry Consultant

Alissa Willmerdinger, MA, LPCA
Mental Health Ministry Consultant

The Catholic Institute for Mental Health Ministry
Department of Counseling and Marital & Family Therapy
University of San Diego

ACKNOWLEDGEMENTS

The Catholic Institute for Mental Health Ministry
Advisory Group

Erika Cameron, PhD, Associate Professor and Chair
Dept of Counseling and Marital & Family Therapy
University of San Diego

Most Reverend John P. Dolan
Auxiliary Bishop of San Diego

Deacon Tom Lambert
Archdiocese of Chicago

Deacon Ed Shoener
Diocese of Scranton

Nicholas Ladany, PhD, Dean (Ex Officio Member)
School of Leadership and Education Sciences
University of San Diego

Our advisory group has consistently provided inspiration, critique, guidance and shared their time abundantly in this work. For that we are truly grateful. We are especially thankful to be blessed by the generosity of Deacon Ed and Ruth Shoener, who from the depths of tragedy and moving in the gifts of the Holy Spirit have supported our work from concept to reality.

As with most project work there are numerous allies, advocates and thought partners that assist all along the way. We would like to specifically acknowledge the pioneering work of the Diocese of San Diego Mental Health Ministry Network and especially the lay Mental Health Ministers in San Diego Parishes that shared their time and experience so graciously with us. We are also appreciative of Jeff Rohling and Bill Ness from eTherapyFinder who have provided much direct support of our efforts and remain our comrades in arms as we continue this work across the country.

TABLE OF CONTENTS

INTRODUCTION

A RATIONALE FOR CATHOLIC MENTAL HEALTH MINISTRY

St. John wrote, "The thief comes only to steal and kill and destroy. I have come so that they may have life and have it to the full." For many Catholics suffering from mental illness the stigma, shame and in some cases shunning they experience creates a barrier to engaging meaningfully in the life of the Church, moving closer to Christ and indeed living life to the full. Our intention in this volume is to compile and present resources for lay ministers and clergy to thoughtfully and effectively implement mental health ministries in dioceses and parishes. Guided by a scholarly review of relevant literature regarding Mental Health Ministry as well as our own fieldwork observing and learning best practices, we offer this resource as a "playbook" to assist our fellow ministers in successfully beginning and developing their ministries. While this work is informed by the scholarly and research literature, we intentionally wrote this in an accessible style typical of instructional texts. This is not meant to be an academic treatise, rather our intention is for our readers to put the content of this volume into practice.

Our work is also guided by the simple and compelling principles outlined in the 2018, *Hope and Healing: A Pastoral Letter from the Bishops of California on Caring for those who Suffer from Mental Illness*. These principles are outlined below.

Principle 1. *Christ calls us to attend to those who suffer from mental illness and provide hope and healing.* With this in mind, the first three chapters of this manual cover the basics of Mental Health Literacy, which we judge to be a necessary requisite for those participating in Mental Health Ministry. Indeed, to attend to those coping with mental health problems, a basic understanding of mental health, common vocabulary and the process to initiate appropriate referrals is required.

Principle 2. *The scope and burden of mental illness in our society is enormous. We are all affected by mental health concerns.* The experience of depression and anxiety are common to our emotional life as humans and how we learn to cope and adapt to these experiences is often a lifelong process. Additionally, the impact of severe mental illness is often either felt directly in our lives or indirectly through the suffering and struggles of a loved one. Mental health problems are common and treatments are available. An active Mental Health Ministry equips the church to help connect parishioners with appropriate referrals as well as to provide prayerful accompaniment as parishioners navigate treatment, crisis and healing.

Principle 3. *Those suffering from mental illness should not be stigmatized or judged. Mental illness remains poorly understood even by clergy and others in positions of influence.* In the healthcare community, mental illness is viewed as having clear neurobiological and genetic correlates, and treatment for most major psychiatric conditions involves both physical as well as psychological components. Mental illness should never be viewed as the consequence of character flaws or lack of faith. Imagine how ridiculous it would be to judge or stigmatize a parishioner with cancer or assume that a lack of faith caused their illness! Yet, we continue to view mental illness as somehow different in its origin. As Catholics, we are called to reach out and embrace all of our brothers and sisters suffering from illnesses, and we need not treat mental illness as different from any other medical condition. Indeed, St. Dymphna is recognized by the Church as patroness of both mental *and* neurological disorders as well as mental health practitioners *and* neurologists.

Principle 4. *The Church, health care professionals and scientific researchers should work together to improve mental health care.* An effective and sustainable response to mental illness in the Church requires a collaborative approach. Here at the Catholic Institute for Mental Health Ministry we recognize that our work to promote Mental Health Ministry necessitates that we engage meaningfully with clergy, laity, researchers and practitioners to advance the notion of Mental Health Ministry in the Church.

Principle 5. *We must meet and attend to those in need where they are.* Our sisters and brothers coping with mental illness are sitting next to us in the pews during Mass as well as sleeping in the Church parking lot at night. This means that we should design outreach efforts to both engage known parishioners more deeply as well as connect our efforts to the community around us. How we organize our ministries will determine our degree of success in these efforts.

Principle 6. *Those impacted by suicide need our compassionate response.* Suicide is tragically a common symptom as well as complication of mental illness. It needs to be understood as such, with no judgement. Instead, many loved ones of decedents from suicide may live with shame or guilt. Therefore, we must respond with embrace, compassion, love and prayer. Our response as compassionate and prayfull companions can help to relieve this unnecessary pain and also make our parishes more welcoming and Spirit-filled communities.

We have organized this volume as a companion to inform the implementation of Mental Health Ministry either at the diocesan or parish level. With that said, the methods outlined in this volume should also apply to the implementation of ministries in other Catholic settings such as schools, colleges and hospitals. Irrespective of setting we emphasize in the first section of this book the importance of a common understanding, vocabulary and specific skills to engage individuals with mental health problems as critically important for an effective ministry. We refer to this as *Mental Health Literacy* and recommend anyone seeking to implement mental health ministries invest the time in completing a basic 8-hour course (i.e., Mental Health First Aid or equivalent) on this topic. We have also learned that the content and resources for ministry activities are an important part of implementing an active and effective ministry. The "middle" of this volume addresses this with specific ideas for spiritual support for those coping with mental illness as well as liturgical considerations and devotions to Saints known as patrons for mental illness or associated with topics closely related to mental health.

The final sections address the structures, processes and progress of ministry implementation. This includes both strategies for internal ministry organization as well as outreach to allies in support of the ministry. How ministry teams evaluate the impact of their ministry is also discussed as an important ongoing aspect of ministry implementation. An important and easily overlooked aspect of ministry implementation that we also address is the stewardship and ongoing support of ministry team members. We assert that attention to ministry stewardship and attention to the self-care of ministry members will facilitate the sustainability of the ministry. We encourage the reader to reflect on how they will implement the ideas and methods described in this volume in a ministry that will support parishioners mental health needs in a Catholic, sustainable, ethical and meaningful way.

1

Recognizing the Signs and Symptoms of Common Mental Illnesses and Substance Use Disorders

In order to build a successful Mental Health Ministry Team a grounded foundation in Mental Health Literacy is key. Mental Health Literacy is simply defined as a person's knowledge and beliefs about mental illness. There are five main components of Mental Health Literacy: (1) recognizing disorders and signs of psychological distress, (2) knowledge of risk factors, causes and interventions, (3) awareness of mental health professional support available to the community, (4) attitudes and beliefs that encourage help-seeking behaviors, and (5) acknowledging when to obtain mental health information and guidance (Compton, Hankerson-Dyson, & Broussard, 2011). Keep in mind a Mental Health Ministry Team is not a clinical team; however, a Mental Health Ministry Team's ability to combine faith-based practice and the use of language, knowledge, and support consistent with Mental Health Literacy can directly influence the attitudes and perceptions surrounding mental health. Essentially, the goal of improving Mental Health Literacy is to promote the reduction of mental illness stigma, encourage conversations around mental illness, and create a safe environment for individuals to share and seek help surrounding their mental illness.

It is important for the Mental Health Ministry Team to practice and increase the use of Mental Health Literacy as Clergy and Ministers are often the "first line of defense" or "first contact" for those suffering from mental illness, and this initial experience can shape an individual's perception of seeking help within the Church and/or seeking help in the community (Vermaas, Green, Haley, & Haddock, 2017 and Wang, Berglund, & Kessler, 2003). Think of the Mental Health Ministry Team as "Gatekeepers" (Mason, Geist, Kuo, Marshall, & Wines, 2016). With research pointing to people of diverse backgrounds identifying help from Clergy or Church communities as more comfortable than seeking direct help from mental health professions, the Mental Health Ministry team has a responsibility to be familiar with a general understanding of common signs and symptoms of mental illness, be able to gather a sense of a presenting concern/issue and risk factors, and have knowledge of local services and community resources.

The National Alliance on Mental Health (NAMI), a nationwide advocacy group for individuals with mental illness and supports education of mental illness, presents common signs and symptoms generally associated with depressive disorders, anxiety disorders, substance use, psychotic disorders, bereavement, family problems and suicide. The charts on the following pages were originally developed by NAMI (2019) and can assist with improving mental health literacy.

Common Signs and Symptoms for Mental Illness

- Excessive worrying or fear
- Feeling excessively sad or low
- Confused thinking or problems concentrating and learning
- Extreme mood changes, including uncontrollable "highs" or feelings of euphoria
- Prolonged or strong feelings of irritability or anger
- Avoiding friends and social activities
- Difficulties understanding or relating to other people
- Changes in sleeping habits or feeling tired and low energy
- Changes in eating habits such as increased hunger or lack of appetite
- Changes in sex drive
- Difficulty perceiving reality (delusions or hallucinations, in which a person experiences and senses things that don't exist in objective reality)
- Inability to perceive changes in one's own feelings, behavior or personality ("lack of insight" or anosognosia)
- Abuse of substances like alcohol or drugs
- Multiple physical ailments without obvious causes (such as headaches, stomach aches, vague and ongoing "aches and pains")
- Inability to carry out daily activities or handle daily problems and stress
- Thinking about suicide

Suicide Risk

- Threats or comments about killing themselves, also known as suicidal ideation, can begin with seemingly harmless thoughts like "I wish I wasn't here" but can become more overt and dangerous
- Increased alcohol and drug use
- Aggressive behavior
- Social withdrawal from friends, family and the community
- Dramatic mood swings
- Talking, writing or thinking about death
- Impulsive or reckless behavior
- Putting their affairs in order and giving away their possessions
- Saying goodbye to friends and family
- Mood shifts from despair to calm
- Planning, possibly by looking around to buy, steal or borrow the tools they need to complete suicide, such as a firearm or prescription medication

As stated before, the Mental Health Ministry does not diagnose and treat mental illness. The purpose of providing Mental Health Literacy is to educate on mental health challenges. The Mental Health Ministry Team needs to be able to provide spiritual support and recognize warning signs of mental illness that need to be treated professionally. Having a general idea of signs and symptoms as well as a basic understanding of what common disorders look like will help teams to know when to appropriately refer and/or encourage professional treatment. Research shows people most often seek

Clergy assistance with the following concerns: depression, anxiety, substance use, bereavement and marital problems. Less sought out, yet equally important, concerns include psychotic disorders and suicide thoughts/attempts. For your knowledge, use the chart below to reference key characteristics of depression, anxiety, substance use, psychotic disorders and bereavement.

From a faith-based or religious perspective, suicidality (i.e., an individual's tendency to experience and/or express suicidal thoughts, gestures, or attempts) is perhaps one of the most daunting aspects of the expression of mental illness. We have described common signs of suicide risk in the table above so that there can be clarity around what suicidality can look like. There is increased societal concern that the occurrence of suicide is on the rise, especially for younger, more diverse populations. The topic cannot be avoided. We understand that death, in and of itself, is a difficult topic to discuss. When an individual takes their own life, the conditions of death and even the grief that follows, is complicated. Simply put, we hope you consider that suicidality and suicide risk are *symptoms* of various mental health disorders, most notably depression. If a person's death were noted to be a result of 'complications from cancer,' we would feel tinges of sorrow and sympathy. If a person's death is described as a result of 'complications from depression,' also known as suicide, we should feel the same and remain wary of any judgments or exclusions. After all, the individual who has taken their own life has most likely suffered enough judgment and exclusion in their life.

To guide your knowledge and pursuit of Mental Health Literacy, we have compiled the following to outline the common mental health disorders that may be witnessed through Mental Health Ministry. Again, the purpose of this is not for you to be prepared to treat mental illness, but so that you can be informed and able to recognize psychiatric disorders as you engage in ministerial relationships and service to others.

Common Psychiatric Disorders, Signs and Symptoms

Depressive Disorders & Related Concerns	Formal Symptoms (DSM-V)*	Signs to Look For
Major Depressive Disorder or Persistent Depressive Disorder ("Depression")	• Feeling sad, empty, or hopeless for most of the day on most days • Reduced interest or pleasure in all or mostly all activities • Fatigue or loss of energy • Feelings of worthlessness • Difficulty concentrating or indecisiveness • Thoughts of death or suicidality (*explained below*)	• Tearfulness or easily upset (people will describe someone as sensitive or reactive) • Isolation (including neglect of responsibilities, withdrawing from or avoiding social interactions) • Changes in appetite (leading to weight loss or weight gain) • Restlessness and agitation (or in others, sluggishness and lethargy) • In children, increased problematic school behaviors

Suicidality	• Thoughts of death • Visions or "fantasies" of death or dying • Desire to die (with or without a plan) • Attempt to take one's life	• Indirect statements: "My life is over;" "I wish things were different;" "Things would be better if I were gone;" "I can't keep going." • Direct statements: "I don't want to live anymore;" "I wish I were dead;" "I want to die." • Careless or reckless behavior despite knowing the consequences • Access to or collecting methods to take one's life
ANXIETY DISORDERS & TRAUMA- AND STRESSOR-RELATED DISORDERS	FORMAL SYMPTOMS (DSM-V)*	SIGNS TO LOOK FOR
Generalized Anxiety Disorder	• Excessive or uncontrollable worry or fear that "something bad will happen"	• Leg shaking • Nail biting or picking

	• Restlessness or feeling "on edge" • Difficulty concentrating - racing thoughts or mind goes blank • Muscle tension • Sleep problems	
Posttraumatic Stress Disorder (PTSD)	• Exposure to actual or threatened death, serious injury, or sexual violence (either personally experiencing, witnessing, or being exposed to trauma) • Reoccurring and uncontrollable disturbing memories • Reactions as if re-experiencing the trauma • Intense distress or reactivity to cues related to the trauma • Concentrated effort to avoid cues related to the trauma	• Social withdrawal • Irritable or angry outbursts • Panic or extreme discomfort with or without known stimuli • Reckless or self-destructive behavior

	• Consistent negative emotional state (fear, anger, guilt, shame) • Feelings of detachment from others • Sleep problems	
SUBSTANCE USE DISORDERS	FORMAL SYMPTOMS (DSM-V)*	SIGNS TO LOOK FOR
Alcohol Use Disorder	• Alcohol is often taken in larger amounts or over a longer period than was intended • Desire or unsuccessful efforts to cut down or control alcohol use • A great deal of time is spent in activities necessary to obtain alcohol, use alcohol, or recover from its effects • Craving, or a strong urge to use alcohol • Recurrent alcohol use in situations in which	• Irritability • Blackouts or loss of recollection during binge drinking episodes • Frequently hungover • Choosing drinking over other responsibilities and obligations • Drinking alone or in secrecy • Becoming isolated and distant from friends and family members • Codependency of loved ones: excessive emotional reliance on disordered person as

	it is physically hazardous • Tolerance, as defined by either: a need for noticeably larger amounts of alcohol to achieve intoxication or desired effect, OR a lowered effect with continued use of the same amount of alcohol • Withdrawal, as evidenced by to following after individual ceases alcohol consumption: trouble sleeping, sweating, nausea, shaking or hand tremors, feeling restless, anxiety	noted by poor boundaries and attempts to control, enable or defend the actions of the individual with substance use disorder
PSYCHOTIC DISORDERS	FORMAL SYMPTOMS (DSM-V)*	SIGNS TO LOOK FOR
Schizophrenia	• Delusions - belief in something false and unlikely despite	• Social withdrawal • Deterioration of personal hygiene

	evidence for the contrary • Hallucinations - sensory perceptions an individual experiences in absence of stimuli • Disorganized speech - tangential, unclear • Decline in daily functioning • Staring, flat facial expression, or appearing "frozen" • Apathy • Disinterest or lack of motivation to participate in activities • Lack of social interest	• Flat, expressionless gaze or low reactivity • Inability to cry or express joy or inappropriate laughter or crying • Oversleeping or insomnia • Forgetful, unable to concentrate
OTHER MENTAL HEALTH ISSUES	**FORMAL SYMPTOMS (DSM-V)***	**SIGNS TO LOOK FOR**
Bereavement	• Mood or changes in functioning or behavior after the loss of close person or loved one	• Depressive symptoms including: sadness, unexpected crying, isolation, changes in appetite

		• Questioning or seeking meaning in life and death • Anger, irritability, or high reactivity (especially in children) • Changes in energy • Thoughts of death or dying
Situational Adjustment	• Emotional or behavioral changes after the experience of an identifiable stressor • Examples of situational stressors can include: loss of job or significant relationship (i.e., divorce), move or relocation with lack of support, change due to medical diagnosis	• Signs of depression or anxiety (as previously noted) • Verbal reactivity • Reckless behavior or changes in inhibition/control •
Family Problems	• Marital concerns including, but not	• Codependency (as previously defined)

	limited to: poor communication, significant financial burdens, difficulty with sexual intimacy or reproductive problems, suspicion of infidelity • Separation or divorce • Concerns for children's problematic behavioral patterns • Miscarriage or death of a child	• Frequent arguing • Unproductive problem solving • Attempts to maintain secrecy • Changes in behavioral patterns - i.e., canceling or avoiding commitments (in children, refusal to attend school)

*Not all diagnostic criteria/symptoms have been listed from the Diagnostic and Statistical Manual of Mental Disorders, 5th Edition (DSM-V; American Psychiatric Association, 2013)

Recognizing signs, symptoms and risk factors can be challenging. Sometimes initial referrals or presenting concerns may not reflect ultimate psychiatric diagnosis. Some presentations may be more direct. For example, substance use problems tend toward substance use disorder. However, other presentations such as anger, agitation, work problems, relational problems can speak towards a variety of psychiatric disorders. Even among highly trained physicians (non-mental health professionals), recognizing the signs and symptoms of mental illnesses can be difficult. Primary care physicians identified psychiatric disorders in their patients with an average 41.5% accuracy (Su, Tsai, Hung, & Chu, 2011). Physicians do not use structured assessments to determine psychiatric disorders, and neither will clergy or ministers. What is important is to recognize and support an individual with a presenting mental illness concern, and follow-through when referral to mental health professionals is necessary.

Chapter 1 Enrichment Activity

For personal and/or team reflection, examine the following questions:

1. "...We hope you consider that suicidality and suicide risk are *symptoms* of various mental health disorders, most notably depression." Reflect on your reactions, perceptions, and beliefs about suicide. Discuss as a group and identify what knowledge needs to be gained to further prepare for working with others experiencing suicidality or who have lost a loved one to suicide.
2. Taking the five components of Mental Health Literacy, rate or assess your own level of literacy.
3. What are potential ways Mental Health Ministry can respond to individuals displaying signs of the common psychiatric disorders outlined in this chapter? (including scripted responses, programmatic planning, and prayer-based interventions)

2

Reducing Stigma, Engaging Appropriately and Respectfully; De-escalating Crisis Situations Safely

Saint Paul reminds us in his first letter to the Corinthians that through our baptism, we are "one body with many parts." Each of us have unique backgrounds, talents, gifts, and knowledge to offer. By embracing diversity as a strength, there can be learning, growth, and authentic fellowship in any ministry program. The same acknowledgment of the multitude of mental health issues is necessary for us to thrive as one body of Christ. However, embracing mental health challenges can be difficult due to biases and beliefs that develop over time. Within the context of a faith-based congregation, some may have difficulty reconciling the omnipotent and healing power of God with the presence and course of disease, especially the often misunderstood and mysterious origins of mental health disorders. It is important, therefore, for Mental Health Ministry Teams to work to address the stigmas surrounding mental health and approach sensitive situations with careful consideration.

As the Mental Health Ministry Team forms, each individual should take the time to identify personal beliefs, attitudes, and mindsets regarding mental health. Each person's background and depth of exposure to a variety of mental health conditions will inform these personal beliefs. Those with lived contact and experience with psychological issues may come in with a perspective that is intimately informed in some areas of mental health, but not fully developed in other areas. As such, it is important for Mental Health Ministry Teams to communicate within the group - to share knowledge, admit concerns, challenge attitudes, and continually grow and develop without limit. The most productive Mental Health Ministry Teams will constantly find themselves doing internal check-ins as individuals and as a group.

Mental Health Literacy is a powerful tool in combating mental health stigma. Making Mental Health Literacy a priority for all ministers and church staff, not just those working within the Mental Health Ministry Team, will ensure that any parishioner accessing church services will find a safe space, therefore potentially improving help-seeking behavior in those with mental health concerns (Campbell & Littleton, 2018). Providing education and distributing information to the whole congregation will also assist in creating an environment and community where mental health misperceptions are challenged. When the parish as one unified church is open to dialogue about mental health, the impact is far-reaching. Because mental health concerns can affect anyone, of any background or culture, having a church-wide and systemic approach to remaining informed about mental health will support Mental Health Ministry in countless ways.

With all clergy, church staff, ministers, and volunteers maintaining basic Mental Health Literacy, and the Mental Health Ministry Team providing more in-depth knowledge and accompaniment, the mental health needs of the church can be addressed. It is known that church-goers, especially those of minority populations, with mental health concerns prefer to seek help from clergy (Vermaas et al., 2017). The same research study identified that in particular, African Americans, Asian Americans, females, the elderly, and veterans may display help-seeking behavior through church venues. While Mental Health Ministry calls us to welcome, embrace, and accompany parishioners of various backgrounds, the Mental Health Ministry Team has a responsibility to pay special attention to these populations for the purpose of anticipating mental health needs and potential referral.

As a team preparing to serve the mental health needs of your church, it is important to remain sensitive and take basic considerations to approach mental health concerns respectfully. For example, language can play a role in supporting Mental Health Ministry efforts and reducing stigma. By simply shifting from identifying someone as 'mentally ill' to saying that someone 'has a mental health disorder' or is 'experiencing mental health difficulties,' negative connotations can be reduced. Above all, a person with a mental health disorder should never be referred to as the diagnosis (e.g., "She's Borderline" or "He's Bipolar"). Such language is both demeaning and inaccurate. A person is never a diagnosis, whether medical or psychological. Ministers should not be afraid to use language that is presented by the person they are serving while providing consistent fact-based information. For example, if a person has a mental health diagnosis, it can be said that the person has depression, which brings a multitude of complicated symptoms, as opposed to simplifying or devaluing the complexity of the person's experience by saying, "They're just depressed." Likewise, someone who has experienced trauma is often labeled as a "victim." This connotes that the person remains injured, broken, or perpetually victimized. In contrast, referring to this person as a "survivor" will empower them to continue in their recovery and success, as well as inspire supporters to treat the person in a strengths-focused manner. There are many language and paradigm shifts that will help your Team create safe, respectful, and welcoming environments for the church community.

Long-Term Care vs. Short-Term Crisis Intervention

As previously stated, research has shown that church-goers are drawn to seek help for mental health needs from clergy and ministers (Vermaas et al., 2017). Church services are not tied to health insurance or health-services bureaucracy. Therefore, parishioners can find immediate assistance for their mental health concerns without the need for prior approval or referral, concern for payments and fees, or the presumed involvement of other agencies. Additionally, especially due to the vows maintained around the sacrament of Reconciliation, people assume that seeking help from clergy comes with a level of confidentiality and therefore proceed to seek help with a sense of security and comfort. Knowing this, Mental Health Ministry Teams should be prepared to respond to those at every stage of help-seeking behavior: those with an immediate crisis and high need for assistance to those who have had or will have a long journey with a chronic or long-term mental health condition.

Those seeking support in later stages of a psychiatric condition (i.e., they or a loved one has a recognized condition, has been diagnosed, and/or has entered treatment for a mental health issue) will be best served through the accompaniment of Mental Health Ministers. By providing a place for vulnerable conversations and informed and intentional responses, the Mental Health Ministry Team can help combat one of the most universal effects of dealing with mental health concerns - the sense of isolation. Those who need long-term support for mental health afflictions may seek spiritual companionship from Mental Health Ministers. It is understandably easy to question God's presence and intention when facing mental health difficulties. Whether it is through faith-based reflection and discussion, attending meetings or groups with those in need, or maintaining prayer intentions, Mental Health Ministry Teams can find many ways to accompany those with long-term mental health needs.

If faced with immediate crisis situations, Mental Health Ministry Teams have much to consider. There may be times when church-goers, feeling most comfortable and confident in finding solace from a minister, come forward with a serious concern or crisis either they or a loved one are facing. A mental health crisis will require careful response depending on the situation. A mental health crisis can be recognized by some of the following signs:

- ❑ Noticeable changes in daily adaptive skills (i.e., eating, sleeping, hygiene, grooming)
- ❑ Increased or sudden isolation or neglect of vital relationships
- ❑ Agitated behavior (i.e., pacing, rapid speech, verbal threats, destroying property)
- ❑ Unpredictable or dramatic mood shifts

- ❑ Harmful or risky behavior directed toward self or others - including binge drinking and drug use
- ❑ Tangential communication (i.e., incoherent, nonlinear speech that can be difficult to follow)
- ❑ Disclosure of recent trauma event - which may be causing physiological and/or emotional distress, or lack of distress that is of equal concern

Mental Health Ministers should recognize when a parishioner displays or describes witnessing these signs of a mental health crisis. It is important for Mental Health Ministers to maintain consistent and intentional responses to these situations. Of equal importance is the ability for a Mental Health Minister to assist others in recognizing a mental health crisis and how to respond. The following describes helpful and unhelpful ways to respond to immediate crisis situations, which can be used by Mental Health Ministers, or be taught to other church staff, ministers, volunteers, or most importantly, concerned parishioners:

Tips for a Productive Response	Signs of a Counterproductive Response
❑ Remain calm: speak slowly, clearly, and confidently ❑ Be mindful of your own nervous behavior (i.e., leg shaking, pacing, abrupt movement) ❑ Use open body language ❑ Encourage the person in crisis to continue talking ❑ Avoid touching, shouting, rambling, and abrupt movements ❑ Listen to understand and paraphrase to reflect hearing ❑ Wait out (the panic, the screaming, etc.),but stay with - remain patient! ❑ Problem-solve in a collaborative manner - not to take away control and responsibility, but to offer partnership ❑ Assure/repeat what the Minister will do next ❑ Encourage person to think of what or who has helped in the past to rely on known resources	❑ Intense questioning ❑ Judgmental, blaming, or sarcastic comments ❑ Making promises ❑ Jumping to conclusions ❑ Immediately over-empathizing can stunt the person's expression and providing a conclusion indicates doing things *for* the person, not *with* them ❑ Immediately problem solving without all of the details can result in a longer or unnecessary process ❑ Displaying fear or passivity (i.e., dancing around the subject of suicide or other overt mental health concern) ❑ Leaving the person alone

❑ Be aware of personal safety, exits, and options for in-the-moment assistance (i.e., another person as a witness or a person who will call for resources/assistance as needed) ❑ Remove audience as needed	

Any Mental Health Literacy trainings held for the Mental Health Ministry Team or other church staff, volunteers, or parishioners, should involve how to recognize mental health crisis situations and how to respond in the most safe and productive ways. Additionally, community mental health resources should be repeatedly displayed - in church bulletins, on the Mental Health Ministry portion of the parish website, etc. - and should include those resources that can provide immediate, emergency assistance. This may include the local crisis intervention helpline, emergency services (to help de-escalate a dangerous situation, provide screening by trained professionals, and/or transport a person to a hospital as needed), or a list of community centers with mental health professionals on staff. Mental Health Ministers are not obligated to provide treatment for these mental health concerns, but Ministers should work to be as informed and prepared for a multitude of situations they may encounter.

CHAPTER 2 ENRICHMENT ACTIVITY

For personal and/or Team reflection, examine the following questions:

1. What strengths, knowledge, and personal experience do I bring to the Ministry Team?
2. What are my "wounds" that I bear and share with others?
3. What disorders or conditions will be most challenging for me to witness or embrace?
4. As a group, discuss and identify what mental health needs are within your means to address.

3

Initiating Timely Referral to Professional Mental Health Providers

Acknowledging the role of collaboration with professional mental health providers will be an essential part of successful Mental Health Ministry programs. Again, Mental Health Ministers should not be expected to *treat* mental health conditions. Collaborating with mental health professionals will encourage help-seeking behavior and will ensure that those seeking help have quality care and treatment, along with the companionship and support of the Mental Health Ministry Team. Ministers and mental health professionals share values that make collaboration a no-brainer: both ministers and mental health professionals act from the desire to serve and help others, both recognize the dignity of the human person, and both value the need for people who are suffering to find personal connection to others (Aten, Boan, Hosey, Topping, Graham & Im, 2013). Mental Health Ministry Teams should recognize when and how to involve mental health professionals out of the best interest of those in need.

Research has been conducted on the mental health-related topics that clergy, in particular, may encounter in their tenure.

According to a survey conducted by Bledsoe and colleagues (2013), the most common mental health-related services clergy felt they were not able to provide included employment/unemployment assistance; LGBTQ (lesbian, gay, bisexual, transgender, and queer) concerns; substance abuse issues; stress and anger management; and legal issues (Aten et al, 2013). As mentioned in Chapter 2, there is much value in a Mental Health Ministry Team reflecting on what is within their scope of knowledge, experience, and skills. If the aforementioned list of mental health-related services align with some of the known needs of your church community, begin finding legitimate resources and sources of information directly related to these topics. As with any church program or ministry, acting from a place of humility is paramount. In the case of Mental Health Ministry, humility looks like reaching out for wisdom and help when needed, and referring to professional mental health treatment providers in a timely manner. Ultimately, acting with humility can be life-saving.

At first, accompanying church community members with mental health concerns may be straightforward and easily done. These church-goers may present with what are called "subclinical" mental health concerns, meaning that their identified symptoms or challenges do not meet criteria necessary to be formally diagnosed and/or they may not be receiving any psychological aid or treatment. For these community members, simply having a conversation or prayer partner may be enough. It is important for Mental Health Ministry Teams to be mindful of complacency when working with these "easy" parishioners. At the same time, Mental Health Ministers should recognize that some people are hesitant to seek and accept professional help due to the stigma behind mental health. As Mental

Health Ministers, there will be a fine balance between encouraging and advocating for someone to seek professional help and allowing people to take steps toward treatment when they are ready. This is why continual dialogue with mental health professionals is necessary for consultation and connection of services. Should the "subclinical" concerns become more than temporary challenges, more severe or have an effect on multiple areas of functioning, Mental Health Ministers should strongly encourage the involvement of professionals (Vermaas et al., 2017). Having pre-established relationships with local resources, support services, and mental health providers will make the referral process easier and streamlined.

You might be pondering, "But how are relationships with support services and mental health professionals even established?" Maybe your parish has no known local resources at the start. Or, your Mental Health Ministry Team may have inherited a list of local mental health providers from your parish records that is dated two or three years, or even a decade old. Creating and maintaining a record of current, legitimate, open mental health resources is paramount. As you look to refer parishioners to professional support, make sure that the professional support maintains a current license in the least, and is willing to take on a new client who may want spirituality incorporated into their treatment.

As a Team, you may consider creating a "Response Protocol" or a guideline of expectations for how to navigate a variety of situations, including but not limited to, immediate de-escalation or crisis situations (as described in Chapter 2) and when/how to refer to mental health professionals. A common and consistent response from all members of the Mental Health Ministry Team, and perhaps extending to the ordained, other ministers, and church staff, will build a stronger program. A shared response will ensure that Mental Health Ministry is providing legitimate support, so all members of the team should acknowledge and agree to refer parishioners to other resources and mental health professionals when presenting with severe mental health concerns or are in crisis (Pillion, Reed & Shetiman, 2012).

Whether it is through the development of formalized protocols or guidelines, holding regular meetings to communicate concerns and seek consultation, or setting aside time to find resources that will meet parishioners at their level of comfort, there can be a variety of ways to support church community members' mental health needs. Incorporating regular trainings and conversations with mental health professionals will improve Mental Health Ministers' knowledge base and improve services. When scheduling trainings prove to be difficult, simply exposing Mental Health Ministers to local agencies, attending free or low-cost local events aimed to improve mental health services or targeting specific populations (i.e., Mental Health Run/Walk), and networking at as many opportunities available will increase the efficacy of the Mental Health Ministry Team. In the end, these local agencies and events can be shared with the church community as resources, either directly or indirectly. That is, Mental Health Ministers can invite parishioners to local mental health-related events, go to a resource center or agency with a church-goer, or make calls and appointments with the person in need as direct service. In a more passive manner, resources and steps for help-seeking can be posted on the parish website to capture those who may not ready to engage with Ministers but are desiring more information. Ultimately, discussing as a

Mental Health Ministry Team what you yourself would want if seeking help - an active companion on the journey, help with referral and seeking treatment, or more passive support - will inform how your Team can proceed to serve the mental health needs of your church.

Chapter 3 Enrichment Activity

For personal and/or Team reflection, examine the following questions:

1. What mental health aspects or issues have you or your parish encountered? Are there common themes of mental health challenges your parishioners face?

2. Considering the population you will serve. What are the "pros and cons" for the following options:

   a. Creating guidelines or a formal protocol for referral to mental health professionals

   b. Holding regular consultation meetings with mental health professionals at the table (to discuss concerns, present questions, learn more, etc.)

   c. Having mental health professionals who are open to "on-the-spot" referrals

3. As a Mental Health Ministry Team (or individual), take a moment to dialogue: what connections to mental health professionals, groups, or agencies do you have that can serve as resources?

4

Differentiating Mental Health Ministry from Mental Health Treatment

As detailed in Chapter 1, Mental Health Literacy involves the recognition of the signs and symptoms of mental health conditions, as well as knowing when to gather more information and seek professional help. Mental Health Ministers must be willing to involve support, information, and guidance from outside sources. As much as the Ministry involves having background knowledge of mental health conditions, in the end, Mental Health Ministry is distinct from mental health *treatment*. The focus of Mental Health Ministry, as with any ministry, should be to journey with others as they experience God and all His works, and to encounter the Trinity in others. Pope Francis has spoken and written about our call as Catholics and Christians to *encounter* or meet others, especially those who are most in need, with grace through Christ. There is a misperception that mental health problems should be treated in secrecy, subsequently increasing the sense of isolation and despair. Ministry has the power to pull people in. As Pope Francis puts it, we are called to go out into the "periphery" and encounter one another. Rarely does mental health treatment trek to these ends. Likewise, rarely does professional treatment ask the question, "Where is God present in this?" or "Where is God in the suffering?" Chapter 8 will explore some theological considerations behind Mental Health Ministry, but as we continue to distinguish ministry from treatment, there is no doubt that the distinction of ministry is that it exists as faith-based and God-centered without direct implementation of psychological interventions.

Mental Health Ministry should be considered a part of the support system necessary for successful professional treatment. A person under the treatment of a mental health professional should be encouraged to find a renewed sense of meaning and purpose, feel grounded in faith or other spiritual practice, and increase social connection as needed - all of which can be found through an active and caring Mental Health Ministry program. Transformation and healing can be a spiritual and ministerial philosophy behind the program. However, to expect that treatment of mental health disorders happen only at a church level - again, treating mental health problems in secrecy - is not embracing of the community and the gifts and talents others may have at addressing mental health issues from an evidence-based approach. Again, we are reminded that we must encounter people as they are, at whatever stage of their mental health journey they may be.

From a psychological perspective, a mental health diagnosis will manifest itself in a pervasive manner, affecting multiple areas of living (i.e., occupational, financial, interpersonal, spiritual, etc.). Given this, sound mental health treatment may involve a number of professionals and support collaborating together - a psychologist or therapist to guide the treatment, a psychiatrist or primary care physician to monitor medication management or any other medical concerns, family and caretakers to provide continual support in the home, and other social supports - such as Mental Health Ministry programs - to share in the everyday journey. Mental Health Ministers provide a spiritual and social support that mental health professionals cannot provide. Treatment can involve theoretical approaches that allow space for making meaning and finding purpose, but the ultimate goal is to address the symptoms and treat the disorder. Ministry, in contrast, has the distinct pleasure of incorporating the all-important existential questions to seek God's will and presence during the hardship.

Across both Mental Health Ministry and mental health treatment, communication and collaboration are necessary. Mental Health Ministry Teams and treatment providers need to come together to acknowledge that there are mental, emotional, physical, behavioral, and spiritual components to mental health. Finding balance and holistic wellness that addresses all of these areas will not be possible without both ministry and treatment co-existing. Treatment may have its limitations - existing in a system of managed care and insurance barriers, not having the freedom to intimately involve faith and religion - but there are methods behind the interventions. Similarly, Mental Health Ministry will have its limitations, but its maintenance as God-centered will undoubtedly contribute to healing and wellness.

CHAPTER 4 ENRICHMENT ACTIVITY

For personal and/or Team reflection, examine the following questions:

1. How have you been nourished by encountering Christ in others through the darkest, most difficult times of your faith journey?
2. Mental Health Ministers provide a spiritual and social support that mental health professionals cannot provide due to therapeutic relationship limitations. Imagine the mental health ministerial relationship - how can you provide spiritual and social support? What questions, comforts, and challenges can you offer to others?

5

Legal and Ethical Issues in Mental Health Ministry: Confidentiality, Historical Trauma and Mandated Reporting

General Ethical and Legal Considerations

As with any ministry or church program, there are ethical considerations that each lay minister or volunteer will be expected to know and understand. A diocese should have "Standards of Conduct" or "Ethical Standards" that outline expectations for all clergy, pastoral counselors, volunteers and lay ministers within that diocese. Additionally, diocese should have a clearly defined scope of duty for lay ministers and volunteers. It is important that anyone who comes forward with a desire to serve on a Mental Health Ministry Team consider a variety of legal and ethical issues that are not only guided by the principles of ministry or the diocese Ethical Standards, but by the sensitive nature of interacting with a person experiencing mental health afflictions. Those Mental Health Ministers who hold active professional licenses or credentials in the mental health field should consider the legal and ethical expectations set by their licensing agency. Although these ministers are volunteers and not formally working in their capacity as a mental health professional, there should be a personal understanding of any moral obligations (or state/licensing agency ethical and legal obligations) that may apply to a variety of situations. Indeed, it is our recommendation that health and mental health practitioners involved in Mental Health Ministry assume roles that support the ministry directly (i.e., organizing, leadership, facilitating large group presentations) but do not necessarily involve individual accompaniment for parishioners. This practice helps limit the potential for dual relationships and confusion of the nature of the lay ministerial relationship on the part of the parishioner. Whether a mental health professional by trade or not, Mental Health Ministers should always maintain appropriate ministerial boundaries and adhere to the scope of duty defined by their diocese.

Given the depth and breadth of information provided in our "playbook," the line between minister and mental health professional can seem convoluted. It might feel like there is so much for a Mental Health Minister to know, consider, and do. However, we must always keep the heart of ministry and the function or purpose of ministry in perspective. While engaging in a ministerial relationship with someone is a personal experience, because of the intimacy of knowing someone's mental health challenges and suffering, it can easily become an enmeshed helping relationship that far exceeds what is appropriate for ministry. The Mental Health Ministry Team should set its own list of expected behavior for its ministers when interacting with the congregation. For example, how will boundaries and limits be communicated? While we have emphasized that Mental Health Ministers should be invested and knowledgeable companions that come alongside others in their journey, it is important to be explicit about when and where Mental Health Ministers can engage with the congregation. For instance, we have suggested that Mental Health Ministers offer to accompany parishioners to community-based support groups or other events that are relevant to mental health support. However, this is within the scope of encountering the congregation on their path to help-seeking. We are not suggesting that Mental Health Ministers extend themselves to all moments of mental health treatment developments. We certainly would not want Mental Health Ministers to feel the need to be "on call" or responsible for immediate communication and companionship. Mental Health Ministers will be in positions to serve, but service still has boundaries. As Saint Paul writes, "Indeed, I worked harder than any of them - though it was not I, but the grace of God that is with me" (1 Corinthians 15:10). That is, the boundaries for serving can be further clarified - it is not the Mental Health Minister at work and providing the grace in this ministry; it is ultimately the work of the Trinity and so the ministerial boundary is simple - do what is humanly reasonable, but allow space for the Trinity to do what it does best.

Boundaries with Minors

A parish's Mental Health Ministry program will need to be firm and clear on its purpose/mission, scope of work, intention, and boundaries or limitations. Mental Health Ministry is not mental health *treatment*; this cannot be emphasized enough. While that limitation is clear, in practice, setting boundaries can be far more challenging, especially when working with the mental health issues of minors. Pope John Paul II was known for his focus on transforming the hearts of the youth through concerted ministry efforts. He is credited with saying that it is a "vocation to love that naturally allows us to draw close to the young." Some Mental Health Ministers may find setting boundaries with minors to be especially challenging as encountering young people with any degree of mental health challenges can spark a great desire to help. In the end, all ministers should be able to manage their emotional reactions and boundaries with any parishioner with whom they may potentially work. Diocesan "Standards of Conduct" or other processes for orienting volunteers and ministers to working with youth will always guide the boundaries set in ministry, especially when working with minors.

Multicultural Considerations

There are many reactions and various levels of receptivity to mental health issues based on beliefs, values and cultures that vary from person to person, family to family, community to community, and so on. Taking a personal inventory of the messages you received throughout your lifetime about mental health, or having serious problems and seeking help, will give you an indication of how perceptions are formed. Your own impressions of mental health may differ greatly from someone with whom you would consider yourself close. Building your self-awareness about your reactions, thoughts, and beliefs about various aspects of mental health, including an honest acceptance of what aspects you feel most drawn toward and what aspects you are most hesitant to encounter, will be a necessary part of building a strong Mental Health Ministry Team. Likewise, communicating these reactions to those on the Mental Health

Ministry Team and continuously opening up about your experience in ministry will help ensure that fulfilling the mission of the Mental Health Ministry team is done with great intention and care.

Just as your own impressions about mental health may have been influenced by culture, those that the Mental Health Ministry Team will serve will also come with perceptions about mental health that have been formed by a multitude of interactions and messages received. There are some general known culturally-influenced attitudes about mental health and related help-seeking behavior. As previously mentioned, when interviewed, those identifying with certain cultures - African Americans and Asian Americans, for example - reportedly prefer to seek support for mental health issues from clergy (Vermaas et al., 2017). Likewise, these populations, along with Latin and Hispanic cultures, tend to mistrust systems of care related to mental health. Some folks, by heritage or lifestyle, prefer natural and holistic approaches to all health issues. It is important to acknowledge how difficult help-seeking for mental health concerns can be for people in general, but especially for those whose culture may stigmatize mental health and its treatment.

Gender and LGBT-related concerns can also impact how parishioners respond to Mental Health Ministry. Definitions of masculinity and gender roles have long been inspected and debated throughout many religions and cultures. There are certainly many within the LGBT community who have their own personal experiences of shame, guilt, and trauma when chastised by members of the church or even members of their own family who have remained staunch in religiosity without any acknowledgment of the compassionate love of Christ we are all called to give. There is a space within Mental Health Ministry for those who have questions, who seek understanding, and are defining their identity or discovering the identity of others and are hoping for the identity of Christian to remain constant.

Responsible Caretaking & Self-Care

Mental Health Ministry can demand for many "considerations" to be made - ethical, legal, multicultural, and more. Because it will take great effort to maintain all of these considerations, Mental Health Ministry Teams have an obligation for consultation with mental health professionals, collaboration with others in Mental Health Ministry, and continued education out of respect for the dignity of those we serve. Through humble admission that Mental Health Ministers do not need to know everything about the world of mental health, we can offer a safe space to learn and grow and experience together. The most responsible caretaking involves responsible accompaniment.

As this chapter emphasizes, boundaries will ensure that proper ministerial relationships exist. However, boundaries are equally important for the balance they can bring Mental Health Ministers on a personal level. Remaining mindful of our own personal well-being as we serve and accompany those that suffer from terrible and sometimes traumatic circumstances and conditions, will keep us from experiencing our own forms of helplessness, depression, and burnout. It is easy to become entwined in the lives - the ups and downs of treatment, recovery and relapse, progress and backslides - of those suffering from mental health challenges. We may think that answering a call to serve as Mental Health Ministers means sacrificing our own selves so that others can begin to find the light, comfort, and companionship they seek. For many, serving as a Mental Health Minister will be a volunteer position - on top of the demands of our occupation, family-life, and other relationships and responsibilities. Entering into a ministerial relationship can become yet another caretaking role for those already providing so much support to others. Be mindful of this before becoming involved in the Mental Health Ministry program and focus on balance, self-care, and setting boundaries to serve others responsibly.

Private vs. Confidential Communication and Mandated Reporting

Research indicates that people seek support from clergy due to the premise of confidentiality (Vermaas et al., 2017). While this research reviewed those in a formal position at the church ("clergy"), it can follow that those who access the Mental Health Ministry program will presume a level of safety and desire for confidentiality. To clarify, there is a distinction between confidential communication and private communication. Private communication refers to information that is not typically shared in public, but is more for the individual or for those closest to the individual to know or witness. Confidential communication usually means that information is personal and permission must be given for that information to be shared. Confidential communication is usually protected by law; private communication may not be clearly protected. In nearly all situations of Mental Health Ministry, communication between parishioners and ministers will be considered private, not confidential.

It should be clarified from the beginning of the ministerial relationship which communication may be considered confidential and which disclosures will remain private , with both confidentiality and privacy clearly defined. Additionally, Mental Health Ministers should explain their scope - their knowledge and abilities/services (i.e., listening, prayer, accompaniment) that they can provide. We are being mindful of these steps to emphasize the responsible services Mental Health Ministers give. As we have covered, people who access Mental Health Ministry may assume that they can receive *treatment* from the church programs or may disclose intimate details of their mental health challenges believing these will be held in confidence. Mental Health Ministry is not treatment. However, to provide a safe space where all are welcome and able to find connection, Mental Health Ministers can assure the congregation that they will be cared for. While clergy (i.e. priests, deacons) may be able to give more clarity around private vs. confidential communications, in the end, please remember that Mental Health Ministers should never mislead.

Mandated Reporting

State statutes defining those to be considered mandated reporters of child abuse and neglect - meaning those with a legal obligation to report any time they suspect child abuse may have occurred historically or is currently occurring - vary from state to state. The laws return to the concept of privileged versus confidential communication in the context of confession. First, it is important to define clergy and their role. In California, "clergy" is defined as priest or "similar functionary of a church" (California Penal Code § 11165.7(a)(32)-(33)). Second, Mental Health Ministry Teams should be attentive to when reporting is mandatory and when it is

Top Level 1-Bay 1-1094

Catholic Mental Health Ministry: Guid
Sku: **4HSLYV001LCR**

Acceptable
Buy with confidence! Comes with our 100% money back guarantee!! Tracking included with every order!!! **** Access codes and supplements are not guaranteed with used items **** This book has markings on the cover .... Cover is showing signs of some creases .... The pages show normal wear ....

Ship To
laura thompson
1917 Stonebridge Dr Apt 1B
New Lenox, IL 60451-2335

Order Details

Order ID	112-0366242-5092226
Order Date	09/26/2023 11:54:07 AM
Shipping Service	Standard
Buyers Name	Laura Thompson

Opalick strives to have each and every customer 100% satisfied with their purchase. If for any reason you are not 100% satisfied please email us at sdafap@yahoo.com with your concerns.

If we need to make something right, we will, Guaranteed!

not. Taking California as the example once more, clergy who reasonably suspect child abuse or neglect as a direct result of "penitential communication" (i.e., confession), which is communicated in confidence, does NOT have to report (Cal. Penal Code § 11166(d)). However, when clergy are "acting in some other capacity that would otherwise make the clergy member a mandated reporter" (i.e., outside confidential communication during confession), they must report suspicion of child abuse or neglect. While volunteers and ministers do not hold the title of "clergy," nor carry all responsibilities and functions of a priest, diocesan Standards of Conduct or similar guidelines may further define the expectations of ministers when it comes to mandated reporting. If it is this clear by state law when a priest is to report suspected child abuse - any time the information is received outside of the confidential communication of confession - then it is likely that whenever a Mental Health Minister suspects child abuse or neglect is occurring or has occurred, they will need to follow the expectation to report this suspicion to local law enforcement or child welfare agencies.

Survivors of Clergy Sexual Misconduct

Dioceses nationwide are creating the infrastructure necessary to address survivors of clergy sexual misconduct, their loved ones, and those clergy involved in sexual misconduct. It is necessary that Mental Health Ministers know the expectations of their diocese when it comes to working with those who disclose being survivors of or having knowledge of acts of sexual misconduct by clergy. Here we will refer to sexual misconduct as terminology to encompass sexual harassment, sexual exploitation, and sexual abuse. Your diocese may clearly define terminology (i.e., sexual misconduct) for you to consider and use when working with others in your capacity as a Mental Health Minister.

The United States Conference of Catholic Bishops (USCCB, 2018) has recently revised its *Charter for the Protection of Children and Young People*, to outline "practical and pastoral steps" focusing on the need to protect the youth of the church, as well as assist in the healing of those affected by clergy sexual misconduct. One such step is to create a safe environment. All clergy, ministers, volunteers, and anyone working in a role of service in a parish must consider the standards of conduct set by the diocese and clarified at the individual parish level. Mental Health Ministers can assist by reminding others to keep their communication open and always create a safe space for dialogue and worship. The Mental Health Ministry Team can also organize an educational series to help youth of all ages learn about personal safety, which the children can apply both at the church and outside of the church. Dialogue as a Team and as a parish for what steps you may need to take in order to protect the young people while they access church services.

For those who have disclosed being survivors or otherwise impacted by clergy sexual misconduct, a focus on healing and reconciliation should be maintained (USCCB, 2018). When responding to a person disclosing they are a survivor of sexual misconduct, or a person whose loved one is a survivor, take the following into consideration:

- As mentioned in Chapter 2, remain calm and refrain from expressing your immediate feelings or reactions (i.e., shock, rage) so as to avoid influencing the survivor's process.

- Allow the survivor to express their range of emotions (i.e., anger, sadness, fear).
- Empower the individual to take action as needed - explain how reporting can be managed if the incident of misconduct has not already been reported, encourage the survivor to seek support from mental health professionals and/or medical care as necessary. It is important for the survivor to hear and be acknowledged for what is in their control.
- Encourage the survivor (and loved ones) to allow authorities, including those at the diocese, to respond.
- If the survivor of sexual misconduct by the clergy is currently under the age of 18, mandated reporting must be followed and legal guardians will need to become involved.

The Mental Health Ministry Team should endorse and help build the strength and resilience of all of their parishioners by encouraging help-seeking behavior and wellness always, but most especially in the case of survivors of clergy sexual misconduct.

A Mental Health Minister who encounters a survivor of clergy sexual misconduct will need to recall the importance of referral. Referral, and sometimes accompaniment with the referral, will need to be made to medical care, diocesan resources (i.e., Diocesan Victims Assistance Coordinator), and mental health professionals as indicated. Respect for the individual and loved ones should also remain a priority. The survivor and their loved ones may have lived years after the incident before allowing others close enough to know their experience. Many who have experienced such a violation have questions, insecurity, and damaging perspectives of religiosity and faith. These boundaries and wounds must be respected as unique to each survivor and/or loved one. The process of recovering and dwelling as a survivor may be tough to understand, but will most desperately require sensitive accompaniment. Mental Health Ministers ought to continue with compassion and a constant sense of welcome, ensuring that the parish is a space where healing and reconciliation can take place.

Chapter 5 Enrichment Activity

For personal and/or Team reflection, examine the following questions:

1. Take time to review the "Standards of Conduct" or other publications specifying the formal expectations for the behavior of all ministers, volunteers, and the like within your diocese.
2. What cultural and/or age-relevant considerations do you foresee as being most sensitive and pertinent in your parish?
3. Rehearse the following (good exercise to do in dyads):
    a. Explain the purpose of the Mental Health Ministry program.
    b. Describe the scope/role of a Mental Health Minister, including limitations and boundaries.
    c. Elaborate on the difference between private and confidential communication.

6

Specialized Mental Health Ministries: Spiritual Support for Severe Mental Illness, Substance Abuse and Chronic Mental Illness

All of the considerations, suggestions, and possibilities explained in this "playbook" thus far may make the work of a Mental Health Ministry program seem daunting. Let us not lose hope. Mental Health Ministry has been successfully implemented in many churches and the benefits have been proven. In particular, Mental Health Ministry has been shown to effectively support church community members with Mood Disorders (i.e., anxiety, depression) (Matsuzaka, Wainberg, Norcini Pala, Hoffman, Coimbra, Braga, and Mello, 2017). Anecdotally, people often turn to God, faith, or religious traditions when they experience suffering, restlessness, disconnect, or longing. Thinking back to the common signs of mental illness outlined in Chapter 1, some of these may be the most common reasons for Mental Health Ministry services. Lay ministers can be useful in assisting with the reduction of depressive symptoms, such as sadness, hopelessness, and finding a sense of worth. Ministers can persuade those with anxiety to identify what is within their control and reduce anxious feelings through centering prayer or spending time in silent reflection. While it may seem like there are many steps and things to consider, Mental Health Ministry can help transform lives, even the lives of those with severe or chronic mental illnesses.

The Mental Health Ministry Team should collaborate with other health and social ministries within the parish to create an inclusive and safe community for those experiencing any level of emotional distress. The overlapping purpose of these ministries is to connect to the parishioners, encountering others as they are and promoting their well-being. By working with other existing ministries, Mental Health Ministers can dive into the service of those with chronic mental health problems. Ideas include sponsoring care packages for those whose loved ones may be going through a particularly difficult time, sharing a rotating visiting schedule for those hospitalized or homebound due to mental health issues, and holding prayer groups or joint-sponsoring devotions. The potential for this collaboration is only limited by the imagination.

Those with major mental health problems (i.e., psychosis, endorsing high suicidality, severe developmental or behavioral concerns) should seek treatment from a mental health professional first and foremost. If it is identified that the severity of the mental health challenge is beyond the scope of what the Mental Health Ministry Team can address, then referral is the highest priority. Once again, we refer back to the definition of Mental Health Literacy as it includes the recognition and knowledge of a variety of mental health conditions, as well as the awareness of supports available and the ability to seek guidance as needed. In the case of more serious mental health concerns, Ministers can provide support in a mixture of ways:

- Offer a comforting, nonjudgmental, and validating space where those with severe challenges and/or their loved ones can feel safe, heard, and supported
- Become educated (by credible sources of course!) and show an interest in their experience of the mental health problem
- Bring them in and include those with severe or chronic mental illness and/or their loved ones
    - What parts of church programs or events need to be adjusted to include those whose mental health symptoms may be exacerbated during the program or event? Is accessing the liturgy a problem because of the severity of their symptoms? What can be accommodated?
- Promote and accompany (if allowed) parishioners to local, professionally-led support groups
- Ask the person with severe or chronic mental illness and/or their loved one what they need, what would best support them, and go from there
- Pray, pray, and pray some more!

There is a place and a purpose for Mental Health Ministry in the support and betterment of the lives of those experiencing severe or chronic mental health challenges and their loved ones.

Consideration for those with Addiction or Substance Use Disorders

Substance use and abuse issues can be difficult to navigate from any perspective. There are many names and phrases - substance abuse, drug or alcohol addiction, chemical dependency, or alcoholism (when specifically dealing with alcohol) - that you may have heard as easily interchangeable terms to describe someone's excessive and patterned use of drugs or alcohol even when faced by significant life problems related to their use. According to the 2017 National Survey on Drug Use and Health sponsored by the Substance Abuse and Mental Health Services Administration or SAMHSA, 19.7 million Americans (ages 12 and older) had a substance use disorder, including 14.5 million Americans who struggled with an alcohol use disorder in particular. The same survey found that 7.6 million Americans (ages 12 to 25) had a major depressive episode in 2017. While the experience of a major depressive episode is a great concern and should receive careful attention, these numbers are shared to point out that while many presume mental health problems are synonymous with depression and anxiety, something like a substance use disorder can be ignored or hidden when clearly, there are many who suffer. It can be argued that many who experience mental health problems may begin to experience problematic and dangerous self-medication (numbing, escaping, or attempting to minimize mental illness symptoms) with substances. Likewise, many with substance use challenges may come to experience substance-induced depression and anxiety, or a slew of other mental health concerns in conjunction with their substance abuse.

There is much information available on the great world wide web regarding substance abuse and chemical dependence. Of these many pearls of wisdom, Mental Health Ministry programs should consider that substance abuse exists as a "family problem" that affects all members of the family, not just the person who has the substance abuse disorder. Addiction can often feel unpredictable - behavioral patterns may exist, but the duration or intensity can vary greatly.

Because of this, along with the constant fluctuation in the person with substance use difficulties being unreliable or failing to carry through with responsibilities, those surrounding the person with substance use problems are often left feeling overburdened, insecure, under-valued, and exhausted. Reaching out to the family, encouraging them to practice self-care and self-love, and showing them compassion will be essential functions of the Mental Health Ministry Team.

Many of those with a substance use disorder and their families find success and support through groups modeled after a 12-Step Program, such as Narcotics Anonymous, Alcoholics Anonymous, or Al-Anon Family Groups. These 12-Step Programs commonly endorse an individual acknowledging that they are powerless to alcohol or substance and should surrender to a "Higher Power." For those connected to a faith tradition, this Higher Power may easily become God in all His omnipotence. While some acknowledge God, in the end, Mental Health Ministers should embrace that the concept of "God" or a Higher Power that is seeker-sensitive. Other processes in 12-Step Programs include self-reflection and acceptance of what actions have been done through the experience of addiction, as well as making amends and seeking forgiveness for many wrongs and hurts. The Mental Health Ministry Team can clearly link to these processes. Mental Health Ministers can listen genuinely to others' experience without judgment, support the reflection process, validate the difficulty in acknowledging and allowing God to be fully in control, and always promote health and safety first and foremost. Many 12-Step Programs begin with a wholehearted acknowledgement of the addict's powerlessness to the substance or compulsive behavior, and the humility to surrender to the will of a

Higher Power. Strip away all titles, diagnoses, and labels and this path simply sounds like a person following the footsteps of God.

CHAPTER 6 ENRICHMENT ACTIVITY

For personal and/or Team reflection, examine the following questions:

1. Take a moment to research: What local support groups, mental health agency events, or 12-Step meetings exist in your neighborhood as potential options for your parishioners?
2. Discuss honestly: What parts of church programs or events need to be adjusted to include those whose mental health symptoms may be exacerbated during the program or event? Is accessing the liturgy a problem because of the severity of their symptoms? What can be accommodated?

7

Liturgical Considerations and Devotions to Saints for Mental Illness

There are many Christians who endorse and live by the words, "When in doubt, pray it out." At this point in our "playbook," Mental Health Ministry may seem "as clear as mud." And so, we fall back on the foundations and core teachings of our church, found in Scripture, the Catechism of the Catholic Church, writings of church leaders such as Pope Francis, and of course the Saints, our role models in faith. Entrusting that God is at work in the lives of the parishioners we serve and seeking the understanding necessary to journey with those suffering from mental illness, will take active prayer. In this chapter, we look at the most simple and basic ways to accompany and provide open programming for Mental Health Ministry.

Importance of Scripture

First, we look to Scripture for wisdom and to help make sense of the difficulties of mental health challenges. There are many themes found in the book of Psalms, but the idea of man being less than or helpless without the power, grace, love, and guidance of God is clear and can be a helpful anchor when working in Mental Health Ministry. Psalms 42 and 43 describe the soul as distressed, acknowledge the human feelings of isolation and depression, and end in seeking and calling upon God, putting hope in God for safety and comfort. Many who regularly experience the challenges of mental illness can identify with the desperation expressed in these Psalms. Has God forgotten them? Is the oppression and burden of mental health issues a message from God? The anguish of living with mental health disorders is indescribable. As Mental Health Ministers, we cannot promise an immediate erasure of the misery. We can, however, remind others to hope in God and never lose sight of God's constant presence, just as the Psalms remind us.

The epistles of Saint Paul are helpful, straightforward challenges for ministers to live and serve with great love, and reminders for parishioners experiencing mental health difficulties to maintain faith even under the most desperate challenges. In the first epistle of Paul to Timothy, we are summoned to "fight the good fight of faith" (1 Timothy 6:12). This rally call can be a good reminder to those accessing Mental Health Ministry services, as well as those working on the Team - life brings many battles, but we are all armed with faith. In Romans chapter 5, Saint Paul reminds us that because of our faith, we are promised the graces of peace and hope through any difficulty. "Suffering produces endurance, and endurance produces character, and character produces hope, and hope does not disappoint us, because God's love has been poured into our hearts" (Romans 5:3-5). It is difficult to make sense of suffering. For those living with the despair that is associated with mental health afflictions, being reminded to have hope and feel God's love is easier said than done. For this reason, Mental Health Ministers cannot just throw out these Scripture passages without being living examples of what it means to have hope and what it looks like to be God's love for others. As Mental Health Ministers, we use faith and grace to receive others with gentleness and "bear one another's burdens" in a way that defeats the isolation of mental illness and strengthens faith - our own and the faith of those we serve (Galatians 6:2).

Worship and Liturgies

To show that Mental Health Ministry is an embraced and incorporated service to others, church services and liturgies should include mention of mental health, not just as a necessary "checklist" item that we need to make sure we mention, but as a truly integrated concept that contributes to the church's diversity and universal identity. In Mass, homilies and intercessions can begin to acknowledge the realities of mental health issues. When we pray for and serve the sick, do we believe this only applies only to physical ailments? To go even further, an annual Mass celebrating and dedicated to people with mental health challenges can be held. We should recognize that mental health is a part of holistic wellness and we should all be praying for the wellness of our brothers and sisters.

Service and the Dignity of the Human Person

Looking at the Catechism of the Catholic Church, we are reminded that serving in ministry is to support "the common good," both locally and universally. Outreach and companionship with those suffering in the darkness of mental health issues is certainly a fulfillment of our social responsibility to support the human person and the social conditions of others. When we consider that as members of the Catholic Church, we join in the universal mission to support what is necessary for human life, which includes the aspect of *health*, we know that providing Mental *Health* Ministry is of high importance.

As we follow the great commandment to love others, we join in solidarity with the conditions in which others are found. Everyone is invited and welcome to "come as you are," and if they come with debilitating depression, history of trauma, life adjustments that rock their core being, or deep anxieties, Mental Health Ministers will be present to serve. To expand on the acknowledgement of the "common good," the Catechism of the Catholic Church explains social justice and the dignity of the human person. Here, the Catechism explains that we can be a "neighbor to others and actively [serve]" others. To connect to another human person can be all that is needed for ministry to succeed. While Mental Health Ministry Teams have many things to consider in order to be responsible and appropriate ministers, the most basic understanding is the need to embrace and support the whole person, including their psychological dignity.

Devotions to the Saints (Examples in Appendix)

While there are many forms of prayer, devotional practices are a unique method to enhance our spiritual life and remember and accompany those we serve in Mental Health Ministry. We have just reviewed Scripture that anchors the idea that we rely on faith to carry us through - faith to guide us as we serve those fighting through mental health issues and faith for those who seek the graces of love, peace, and hope through their mental health challenges. Devotions to the saints enrich our faith and spirituality. Prayerful times of devotion are simple ways to implement Mental Health Ministry services and can be accessible to everyone, even those who cannot physically reach the church grounds. If there is anywhere to start with programming for a Mental Health Ministry Team, scheduled devotions - offering masses with special intentions for parishioners in need or with the intention of those experiencing mental health difficulties, novenas or prayer times - exposing all parishioners to Mental Health Ministry is a strong way to start.

The patron saint of mental and neurological disorders is Saint Dymphna, whose feast day is honored on May 15. A martyr, the story of Saint Dymphna is one of bold faith and unending courage, fitting graces to seek for those who regularly battle mental health issues. Mental Health Ministry Teams can consider distributing Saint Dymphna prayer cards as an initial outreach to promote the ministry. Another great woman of faith, Saint Monica of Hippo, remained steadfast in her faith as she became a great example and witness of God's love and omnipotence. Saint Monica is revered as the patron saint of abuse victims and is often remembered as someone who constantly prayed for those around her, even her enemies. Petitions and devotions to these great saints can focus on specific mental health disorders or aspects, or may be more generally intended for any emotional and psychological affliction. Prayerful intention can be a steady foundation for Mental Health Ministry.

It is easy to forget the powerful role models we have in the saints. We make modern-day saints and idols of leaders, public figures, or "influencers" who may bring goodness in the midst of the chaos, hustle, and nonsensical cruelties of our current world. While this may give us temporary relief from the trials of everyday life, Mental

Health Ministry includes the challenge to ask the toughest question of those who have abstract ailments - amid the pangs of living with mental health disorders, where is God? The answer can only be revealed through faith and prayer. Sitting with prayerful attention to the saints, whomever we direct our devotions to, will inspire productive accompaniment.

Chapter 7 Enrichment Activity

For personal and/or Team reflection, examine the following questions:

1. What Scripture passages have been a source of comfort for you? What Scripture can the Mental Health Ministry Team adopt as their "power verse?"
2. A great resource to consider creating and providing for those accessing Mental Health Ministry services is a list of Bible verses that are relevant for different mental health aspects. Many online resources exist (as well as an example in the Appendix), but making a list unique to your parish population is personal. Take some time to identify Scripture and associated mental health themes that would be beneficial for your parishioners.

8

Steps to Implementing Mental Health Ministry

By now, our hope is that you have learned, absorbed, and reflected on many aspects of mental health as it is folded into a unique ministry to serve the Church. However, many of you may have been itching to find out just exactly how all of this comes together. As with the rest of this "playbook," the following is based on research and lived experience, but is in no way a perfect recipe for a successful Mental Health Ministry program. Keep in mind that our suggested implementation plan should be adapted to fit the needs of your specific diocese and the parishes it serves and in consideration of your resources and local community context. Five of the six implementation steps outlined below are from Creating Caring Congregations, a five step program developed by the Reverend Susan Gregg-Schroeder (n.d.), an ordained Methodist Minister and early pioneer in Mental Health Ministry. We have added a sixth step, Evaluation, to provide guidance on the how ministry teams can assess the depth and impact of Mental Health Ministry Implementation. All in all, keep in mind the broad concept that in order to build a successful Mental Health Ministry, there must be Awareness, Acceptance, and Accompaniment.

Step One: Education

All clergy, church staff, ministers, and the Mental Health Ministry Team should meet Mental Health Literacy standards so that no matter who comes in contact with a person struggling with a mental health concern, the need for support can be identified in a timely manner. Because Mental Health Literacy begins with recognizing disorders and signs of psychological distress, and having knowledge about the risk factors, causes, and interventions for a variety of mental health conditions, it makes sense to begin the implementation of Mental Health Ministry with education. Education should come from valid and credible sources: survey, interview, and dialogue with mental health professionals in your congregation; identify and visit local agencies or psychiatric hospitals to learn about their programs; read and share information. When turning to print material (i.e., books) or internet articles, make sure that the credentials and background of the author is trustworthy. Many renowned universities and government agencies publish scientifically supported information that can be useful to the Mental Health Ministry Team and congregation. There are many small ways to obtain dependable, and often free, education material.

Of course, if it is within the means of your church, turning to conferences, workshops, or webinars for education opportunities could also be an option. Speakers and experts can be invited in to educate both the Mental Health Ministers, church staff and clergy, and members of the congregation, depending on the topic. There should be a distinction, however, between education provided to Mental Health Ministers and education provided to the general church community given that Mental Health Ministers should be held to higher standards of foundational knowledge. Education for the congregation can be provided through Mental Health Ministry events and resources (including support groups and community-based services) and passive education material (i.e., pamphlets available in the church office, comprehensive electronic resources linked to parish website). Finally, if the church hosts health and wellness events, Mental Health Ministry should certainly be included and allowed to provide education in addition to promotion of their program.

While education is being presented as the "first step" in forming a Mental Health Ministry program, education should always be a part of the ministry. Just as mental health professionals must stay up-to-date on the latest research and progressive considerations, Mental Health Ministers will be expected to continually seek out opportunities for sound learning and useful dialogue. Working with other parishes will be discussed in the final chapter, but sharing wisdom and best practices with each other - across ministries and churches - will be an invaluable way to learn and grow your parish's Mental Health Ministry program.

Step Two: Covenant

Any ministry program will involve commitment - commitment of time, energy, and resources. Additionally, any ministry program will have a basic agreement to serve as we are called, to share the Gospel message, and to act as Christ showed us. Mental Health Ministry will be no exception. The covenant set will last beyond the initial implementation of the program. The commitment within Mental Health Ministry will be unique to the church community's needs, but the heart of service will never change. To help make sure the covenant and purpose is clear, Mental Health Ministry Teams may consider publishing job descriptions or clear lists of roles and responsibilities, qualifications and skills, as shown in our Appendix.

Because of the relative novelty of Mental Health Ministry programs within Roman Catholic communities, it will be important for a clear articulation of the "what" and the "how" of your parish's Mental Health Ministry program. What is the commitment and how will it be achieved? This will clarify and inform the commitment your ministers are making, and help the congregation understand the purpose of the ministry and what to expect. To accomplish this, you may consider creating a Mental Health Ministry Mission Statement, to be explicit about the purpose of the ministry and what you all promise to work toward as a community. Alternate or additional options include creating spaces on the parish bulletin, website, and social media outlets to expose the congregation to the ministry's presence and purpose. However the covenant is established and publicized, each individual Mental Health Minister and the Team as a whole will need to understand, accept, and work to fulfill the commitment.

Covenant requires follow-through. The Mental Health Ministry Team must enact the mission to which they agree. From education to evaluation, there is a renewed commitment along every step of the implementation. Additionally, from day-to-day, there should be follow-through so that the promise is fulfilled. Seek learning; network and collaborate with mental health professionals and local agencies; be active ministers; create events that will support the mental health needs of the church; connect and advocate for the best interest of the church community; and, be open to evaluation and evolution as the world of mental health and the makeup of the congregation continue to change. A balanced Mental Health Ministry team will utilize the strengths and styles of each of their members, and will put these strengths to action. Covenant means action.

Step Three: Welcome

Who will we serve? Everyone. As the Mental Health Ministry Team begins its service, it may or may not be clear who the audience will be. The ministry is open to anyone experiencing mental health problems and their family members, caretakers, and loved ones who may be impacted by the person's mental health challenges. This means that ministers can expect to encounter people coping with their own symptoms and concerns, as well as those struggling with the challenges a mental health diagnosis has brought on the family, partnership, friendship, or even workplace. Everyone should be radically welcome, including church-goers and those who are already active in other church ministries or programs. The church's Hospitality Team (i.e., greeters, ushers, etc.) can be trained on how to welcome *all* congregation members and all church staff, volunteers, and ministers should be aware of the Mental Health Ministry services. Again, mental health issues affect people of all backgrounds and demographics, so there should be no exclusion on who can be included in the ministry.

As was mentioned before, mental health problems can bring up a sense of isolation - the person with the mental health issues feels that no one understands; the person close to someone with a mental health condition fears judgment and feels helpless. By welcoming and embracing everyone into Mental Health Ministry, there is a chance to work against the isolation and provide gentle companionship to all. Consider times where ministers can accompany those with mental health problems and their loved ones: during Mass so that they can encounter Christ through the Liturgy, at church functions so they can feel a part of the community, and during other celebrations and special events to journey with the seasons of the church. Accompanying and welcoming can happen outside of the church grounds too, by going to local mental health agencies or joining them at functions that support their wellness and growth. Any opportunity to be a companion for congregation members experiencing mental health problems and/or their family and loved ones, is a chance for learning, healing, and treatment.

Mental Health Ministers should also be prepared to embrace difficult times. Parishioners with mental health conditions or their loved ones may experience hospitalizations, enter/exit intensive treatment programs, relapse, or have sudden/rapid decline in functioning. The Ministry should continue to welcome, remembering again that we are all one body in Christ. Because of the stigma and presumed judgment behind severe mental health issues, these serious times are often not shared with others - those suffering from a mental health condition and their loved ones must carry on as if nothing is happening, or they may be treated differently. For example, if a neighbor sees the police at a home because someone has just been in a serious car accident, the neighbor might pour out sympathy and even offer help around the house. If a neighbor sees the police at a home because of someone's suicidality, they might gawk, close their doors and shutters, or question what is "wrong" with the person. In the case of hospitalizations, what would be the difference between someone being hospitalized due to complications from cancer or diabetes, and someone being hospitalized due to complications from Bipolar Disorder or Substance Use Disorder? While this may not be true in every case, the person with a mental health issue and/or their loved ones might fear or even experience that this is their reality. During these times, the welcoming presence of Mental Health Ministers will be most dire.

As previously mentioned, creating a safe and inclusive environment where vulnerability and authenticity are welcomed, will make a difference in how the Mental Health Ministry program is received. When parishioners identify Mental Health Ministry as a program where support, emotional security, resources, and accompaniment are all provided, then the ministry is on target.

Step Four: Support

Through open brainstorming and consideration of what is feasible and suitable for your congregation, the Mental Health Ministry Team can create many different avenues by which support can be provided to those with mental health challenges and their loved ones. Mental Health Ministry is a ministry for everyone and buy-in is necessary from the top down, and the bottom up. By creating programs and dialogues where everyone is on an equal plane, we are reaching across to one another to facilitate a successful and transformative ministry. Here we offer some basic ideas that can be implemented as you see fit.

Mental Health Ministry Family Nights - Some churches may already have programming for "Faith and Family Nights" or other opportunities for families to come together in directed and guided faith-based events. Mental Health Ministry Family Nights can be an adaptation of these nights, with a focus still on programming that brings the family closer together in a faith-context. The difference would be in the level of sensitivity Mental Health Ministry Family Nights would have for the needs of those experiencing mental health problems and their families. There can be stand-alone Mental Health Ministry Family Nights:

- ❑ Educational nights can provide information and opportunities for having the "tough conversations" families tend to avoid
- ❑ Witness stories and resources can be candidly shared to help others know they are not alone
- ❑ Movies that build family values or incorporate aspects of mental health can be screened for everyone

Ask your congregation; those in need can best identify the help they seek. If stand-alone events do not seem reasonable, accomodations can be made at any church-sponsored event to ensure that members of the congregation who are dealing with mental illness in one way or another are respectfully incorporated:

- Accomodations for children with developmental or behavioral needs can be made (i.e., less visual and/or auditory stimulation) so that everyone can joyfully participate in different church events
- A clear agenda or opportunities for quiet or individual time (not all mingling and unstructured) would help those with anxiety

Finding ways to make already established church events sensitive to those with mental health problems could be an easy place to start as your Mental Health Ministry Team decides what programs to sponsor.

Active Outreach - Mental Health Ministry may not receive a flood of people coming forward for support and services, and understandably so. As previously mentioned, it can be difficult to acknowledge symptoms and admit to the struggle and impact of mental health problems. It will be imperative for Mental Health Ministry Teams to be prepared to reach out, in careful and sensitive ways. Realistically, those with severe, chronic, or declining mental health conditions may not be attending Mass, prayer services, or other church events. As the Mental Health Ministry progresses and develops a reputation, some of these individuals will come forward. However, with active outreach incorporated as everyone's responsibility, more contact can be made. Other ministers, volunteers, and leaders in your parish can make referrals to the Mental Health Ministry Team when they believe someone can benefit from connecting with the Team. They can refer everyone from those directly experiencing mental health problems, to family members who may be coping with a loved one's new diagnosis, worsening of symptoms, or any other adjustment to mental health conditions. This is why it would be important for everyone connected to the church - from congregation to leadership - to have a clear understanding of the services and mission of the Mental Health Ministry Team, so that help-seeking behavior is encouraged and accomplished.

Active outreach can take place within the church grounds, but also out in the community. As mentioned in the "Welcome" implementation step, just as someone would be visited if they were hospitalized for a complication from a medical condition, Mental

Health Ministers can consider reaching out by visiting those that have been hospitalized due to complications from their mental health condition. The church's Extraordinary Ministers can be sure to coordinate and include those hospitalized or "shut-in" because of mental health conditions in the distribution of the Eucharist. A Mental Health Ministry Team that is visible both at the church and out in the community has a strong potential to make a difference.

Support Groups or Meetings - Many of you may have participated in or have a vision of what a support group can look like: people with some common interest or problem sitting in a circle of chairs in a nondescript room sharing answers and stories as prompted by a facilitator. This is, in fact, not far from reality. Mental Health Ministry Teams should consider the power of offering support groups or meetings to the congregation. Support groups and meetings have the potential to bring people out of isolation, empower groups of people to initiate growth and transformation, can supplement the progress of someone experiencing mental health issues, and their loved ones can find validation and solace. Support groups, however, cannot simply be facilitated by any volunteer or Mental Health Minister. Specialized training and practice would be needed to understand how to manage group dynamics, how to respond to delicate or escalated situations, how to manage participants, how to properly start and end the group, and so much more. For this reason, an alternate suggestion is to offer the church facilities (i.e., multipurpose rooms) to organizations with trained facilitators who are in need of a home. For example, 12-Step Programs could be allowed to use a room once each week at a set time. While this can be limited to members of the congregation only, it could be an "open" group or meeting that brings in new people and spreads the reach of the Mental Health Ministry program. These support groups could be run on rotating series, so that for 8-12 weeks at a time, one support group or meeting could be held with a specific topic, and then the topic or emphasis could change for the next series. Should the Mental Health Ministry program at the church begin to thrive, many groups or meetings could be held simultaneously and the impact would be remarkable.

If the coordination of hosting support groups or meetings at the church facilities proves to be a daunting or a less than thriving venture, Mental Health Ministers can attend community-based support groups or meetings with those interested. For example, a local agency may be hosting a grief support group for families who have lost a loved one to suicide, and supporters are welcome. The Mental Health Ministry program can promote this opportunity and offer to accompany anyone interested to the support group on an ongoing basis. Many support groups or meetings allow "supporters" to attend - someone who is companioning an attendee but does not necessarily need to participate or is looking to benefit from the service. For instance, a supporter attends the grief support group from the previous example, but may not be experiencing grief themselves; they are simply in attendance to help encourage the person they are accompanying. Mental Health Ministers acting as supporters at nearby support groups or meetings has the potential to empower the congregation to access services and support they would not otherwise seek or feel comfortable accepting on their own.

Resources and Referrals - An essential aspect of offering support to those experiencing mental health difficulties and their loved ones is to assist in the navigation of the many resources and agencies available. Supporting someone as they find, attempt to access, and accept services or assistance from a resource has the potential to be a full-time job in and of itself. However, as has been mentioned in various parts of this manual, providing a robust listing of local mental health agencies/professionals or other resources on the church website, bulletin, or other forms of social media and communication will be a simple but powerful way to offer support and ministry to others.

Step Five: Advocacy

The very wise St. Teresa of Calcutta is credited with telling us, "Prayer in action is love. Love in action is service." To take this concept one challenge further, service in action is advocacy. Ministry is a call to service, and without advocacy - taking fellowship and accompaniment into an active supporting role - ministry can become complacent, accepting the way things are and never venturing into new arenas. Without advocacy, the congregation we serve may continue to find limitations to the support they desperately need. The field of mental health is synonymous with advocacy given layers of bureaucracy and the intersection of many systems. Advocacy, therefore, will be an essential step of Mental Health Ministry, putting our service into action.

Within the church, advocacy can take the form of embracing the skeptics. There are many who will question why Mental Health Ministry is necessary, and will challenge whether Mental Health Ministry should be a parish-funded service. Again, it is imperative that Education and Covenant are strongly incorporated into Mental Health Ministry as a foundation to the program. Ministers will need to embrace discomfort and acknowledge they are not necessarily experts in the field of mental health. It is understandably despairing to be challenged or questioned when all we want to do is help those in need. As opposed to embracing defeat, have faith. Pray through the doubt and know that advocacy will look like continuing to serve, continuing to learn, continuing to encounter, and continuing to hope - because this is what those with mental health challenges need the most.

Advocacy will also require reaching out. Because Mental Health Ministry is still developing within the Catholic Church, much of the necessary information and even programming will come from outside. Encourage your congregation to participate in mental health events sponsored in the nearby community. Many cities throughout the United States have local organizations that are dedicated to raising awareness and providing education around mental health issues. There can be local "walks," conferences, or "mental health fairs," that Mental Health Ministers and congregation can benefit from attending. For example, creating a team for the local mental health related 5K walk/run can be an active way (literally) to be in solidarity with those experiencing mental health concerns. When programming at the church feels like you are creating too much from scratch, look outside of the church and partner with others to keep the Mental Health Ministry program vibrant and diverse. Hosting a "mental health fair" on church grounds by inviting local agencies or groups who want to connect with others experiencing mental health issues can be a great way to advance the Mental Health Ministry program and continue to spread awareness and fight stigma surrounding mental illness.

Networking is another way that advocacy can be woven into Mental Health Ministry. Connecting with other Mental Health

Ministry Teams at other parishes, and dialoguing with mental health professionals to know what others are facing- questions, trends, barriers, and successes - will enrich the Mental Health Ministry program. Regular collaboration with mental health professionals will not only ensure ongoing education, it can help Ministry Teams understand what barriers to mental health care exist and what options for treatment are available. Advocacy in the form of communicating to mental health professionals about spiritual considerations can also transform the treatment they are providing.

Step Six: Evaluation

The success of the Mental Health Ministry can be measured by the degree or depth of implementation. We propose a tiered method for evaluating the depth of implementation detailed in the Mental Health Ministry Implementation Matrix (MHMIM) beginning on page 80. Each Tier can also be thought of as a year in the life of the ministry with an overall span of three years for full ministry implementation. The MHMIM is a tool designed for self-evaluation and can be used biannually (e.g., every 6 months) by both parish-level ministry teams as well as diocesan-level ministry coordinators, organizers or directors. The MHMIM score ranges are explained in the table on the next page.

Mental Health Ministry Implementation Matrix (MHMIM) Scoring Table

Implementation Level	MHMIM Score Range	Benchmark Tier/Year
Deep	20-24	Tier 3/Year 3
Moderate	16-19	Tier 2/Year 2
Beginning	15 and below	Tier 1/Year 1

MENTAL HEALTH MINISTRY IMPLEMENTATION MATRIX: *THIS MATRIX IS DESIGNED AS A SELF-ASSESSMENT AND PROGRESS MONITORING TOOL TO EVALUATE THE DEPTH OF IMPLEMENTATION FOR MENTAL HEALTH* ***MINISTRIES.*** (ABBREVIATIONS: HIPAA=HEALTH INSURANCE PORTABILITY AND ACCOUNTABILITY ACT; MHM=MENTAL HEALTH MINISTRY):

Criterion (Score 0 if element is absent)	Tier 1 - Beginning Implementation (1 point)	Tier 2 - Moderate Implementation (2 points)	Tier 3 - Deep Implementation (3 points)	Score
1. Mental Health First Aid Training	Ministry Leader Only	Most team members certified	Requirement to serve on Mental Health Ministry team	
2. Documentation of Implementation	None	Minimal record of ministry work	Articulated, detailed, organized	
3. Evidence of Impact	None	Minimal evidence of ministry impact (i.e., numbers of events held per year and attendance data)	There is systematically collected qualitative and quantitative evidence of ministry impact. This evidence may include focus group data, survey data as well as external indicators such as changes in Mass attendance or measures of	

			parish social climate	
4. Mental Health Ministry Support/Outreach	Fewer than 4 events per year	Between 4 and 11 events per year	Monthly Events	
5. Accompaniment and Direct Support	Non-specific to MHM (clergy and/or lay ministers may be available for accompaniment)	MHM team members provide on an as needed basis	Specific MHM team members are identified to facilitate support groups and are also providing individual accompaniment	
6. Fiscal Sustainability/Budget	None or time-limited funding (i.e., grant or gift)	Time-limited funding stream with minimal records of budget	Articulated budget with reliable funding streams to ensure sustainability of Ministry activities after expiration of grant or gifts	
7. Provider Referral System/Network	MHM team has identified local providers and makes appropriate referrals	Some referral communications are within a secure, HIPAA compliant system	All referral communications are within a secure, HIPAA compliant system. Providers are vetted and respect Catholic beliefs.	

8. Pastoral Support	Pastor is aware of the ministry	Pastor is supportive of the ministry, attending up to 3 meetings or events per year	Pastor is fully engaged in the ministry, attending up to 6 meeting or events per year and speaks on behalf of the ministry at events or from the pulpit	
			TOTAL	

The MHMIM can also be used as a template for the Mental Health Ministry's implementation plan, with each criterion included as a marker assigned a specific month and year to be implemented over the course of three years. The implementation plan should be developed by the Mental Health Ministry Team and each criterion should be assigned to a team member (as part of that member's role) for implementation.

Chapter 8 Enrichment Activity

For personal and/or Team reflection, examine the following questions:

1. Determine an implementation timeline - with clear deadlines - that is realistic for your parish.
2. To ensure fidelity and efficacy, assign different members of the Mental Health Ministry Leadership Team one of the six implementation steps identified in this chapter. Consider holding a retreat or planning day for the MHM Leadership Team to plan goals, objectives, and action items.

9

Leveraging Technology to Support the Mental Health Ministry

Many dioceses and churches throughout the United States have embraced the "mobilization" of ministry through the incorporation of technological platforms. There is no doubt that we are embedded in an age where accessing information is expected to be quick and "user-friendly" given the tiny computers many of us use as cell phones these days. Levering technology to support any church effort can seem daunting and time-consuming. Keeping up with business-related emails could be a part-time position alone in many parishes! Whatever level of comfort you or your parish has with incorporating technology into ministry programs, our suggestions here for using technology to support Mental Health Ministry will not require a full technology support team, guaranteed.

As previously mentioned, explaining the purpose and services of the Mental Health Ministry Team will be essential to harnessing the buy-in of the congregation. Repeating this in the weekly printed bulletin will not only take away prime real estate from other church ministries, but the constant inundation could breed complacency and the valuable ministry could be ignored. By posting the Mental

Health Ministry's mission and list of services on the parish website, whether it is through a special article or a webpage of its own, there can be a single platform to which people can be directed for more information. As the ministry develops, the webpage can become more robust, including links to mental health resources or referrals for local agencies and mental health professionals who may be able to assist with a variety of mental health conditions. There is much potential in maintaining a Mental Health Ministry-specific webpage. But, if this is not within the means of your specific parish, having semi-frequent parish website postings by the Pastor or other ministers announcing some of the Mental Health Ministry's offerings will still catch attention and spread the word.

If possible, a Mental Health Ministry-specific email address could be one of the main methods for leveraging technology to support the ministry. Many inquiries, information requests, or even conversations can be fielded through a Mental Health Ministry-specific email address. There would need to be some coordination behind who would receive and respond to any electronic communication - would it be one point-person or the whole Mental Health Ministry Team's responsibility - but the existence of the email address would support and streamline communication with the congregation and collaboration with mental health professionals, agencies, and other parishes. Another consideration when utilizing a central email address is the timeliness of communication. A parishioner may use email as a means to communicate distress or an emerging mental health crisis. If this is the case, checking the Mental Health Ministry email address once a week, while this may prove sufficient at first, could result in a lapse in providing timely ministry and support to someone in need. Mind you, neither the Mental

Health Ministry webpage nor email address should be promoted as a means to receive direct and immediate mental health support.

Electronic communication can be used to inform and educate the congregation to ultimately build awareness about mental health and combat stigma and misperceptions. As stated in previous chapters, providing accurate and up-to-date information can help those who question Mental Health Ministry feel more comfortable with its validity and can increase help-seeking behavior. In particular, technology has the potential to reach those who otherwise may not access ministry services at the physical church and provides a platform for collaboration and consultation with mental health providers (Javadi, Feldhaus, Mancuso, & Ghaffar, 2017). Voluntary help-seeking is difficult for many people who are in need of mental health services. The idea of walking up to someone and admitting mental health concerns can be intimidating. Communicating with a Mental Health Minister via email or gathering information through online sources linked to the parish website could be more of an attainable first step for finding mental health support. By properly leveraging technology, Mental Health Ministry can build connections with the congregation and will take another step in fighting isolation and mental health stigmas. With this in mind, it is important to not share sensitive personal mental health information about parishioners in need of referrals with other ministry team members or in a referral to a provider over a standard email system or other non-secure means (i.e., texting, IMS or social media direct messaging). It is strongly recommended that diocese and parish use secure, HIPAA (Health Insurance Portability and Accountability Act) compliant systems for such purposes. Indeed some systems offer functionality to organize referral groups and vet the licensure status of mental health providers, and often at no cost to the diocese or parish.

Again, whatever technological effort is possible given the means and circumstances of your church will be another mental health support that may not have previously existed for your congregation. You can start small - creating an email address - and see how the congregation responds. As the Mental Health Ministry Team builds services and credibility, the use of technology can progress as well. However, incorporating some form of online presence from the very beginning will ensure that the Mental Health Ministry is an embedded part of your church's listed ministries and will help in the promotion of the services. It was previously explained that the congregation should be surveyed to learn what mental health needs exist in the parish and identify direct mental health topics that could be addressed in strategic ways. Would it be possible to survey your congregation via online or email survey? If not at first, would this be a helpful communication tool for Mental Health Ministry and all ministries involved at the parish? While incorporating technology can seem unnecessarily taxing, it will prove to be beneficial. Mental Health Ministry's use of technology can disseminate appropriate information, can transform help-seeking behavior by those hesitant to access face-to-face services at first, and can be a model of openness to emerging thinking and ministry. When so much of social media and online communication is contrived, glamorized, secular, and politicized, Mental Health Ministry's authentic communication can be a powerful voice of compassion and hope.

Chapter 9 Enrichment Activity

For personal and/or Team reflection, examine the following questions:

1. Do a quick internet search of any mental health related topic (i.e., "help for anxiety") and note the plethora of results. Independent help-seeking can be discouraging and overwhelming. Taking this perspective, what can your Mental Health Ministry Team do to leverage streamlined and direct technology services to your constituents?

REFERENCES

American Psychiatric Association. (2013). Diagnostic and statistical manual of mental disorders (5th ed.). Washington, DC: Author.

Aten, J. D., Boan, D. M., Hosey, J. M., Topping, S., Graham, A., & Im, H. (2013). Building capacity for responding to disaster emotional and spiritual needs: A clergy, academic, and mental health partnership model (CAMP). Psychological Trauma: Theory, Research, Practice, And Policy, 5(6), 591-600. doi:10.1037/a0030041

Bledsoe, T. S., Setterlund, K., Adams, C. J., Fok-Trela, A., & Connolly, M. (2013). Addressing pastoral knowledge and attitudes about clergy/mental health practitioner collaboration. Social Work & Christianity, 40(1), 23-45.

Buttorff, C., Hock, R. S., Weiss, H. A., Naik, S., Araya, R., Kirkwood, B. R., & ... Patel, V. (2012). Economic evaluation of a task-shifting intervention for common mental disorders in India. Bulletin Of The World Health Organization, 90(11), 813-821. doi:10.2471/BLT.12.104133

California Catholic Conference. (2018). Hope and healing: A pastoral letter from the Bishops of California on caring for those who suffer from mental illness addressed to all Catholics and people of goodwill. Retrieved from https://www.cacatholic.org/hope_and_healing

Campbell, R. D., & Littleton, T. (2018). Mental health counselling in the Black American church: Reflections and recommendations from counsellors serving in a counselling ministry. Mental Health, Religion & Culture, doi:10.1080/13674676.2018.1494704

Compton, M. T., Hankerson-Dyson, D., & Broussard, B. (2011). Development, item analysis, and initial reliability and validity of a multiple-choice knowledge of mental illnesses test for lay samples. Psychiatry Research, 189(1), 141–148.

Furnham, A., Gee, M., & Weis, L. (2016). Knowledge of mental illnesses: Two studies using a new test. Psychiatry Research, 244, 363–369.

Gregg-Schroeder, S. (n.d). Creating caring congregations - five step program. Retrieved from http://www.mentalhealthministries.net/resources/caring_congregations_model.html

Gregg-Schroeder, S., & Nemec, P. (2007). Mental health ministries. Psychiatric Rehabilitation Journal, 30(4), 315-317. doi:10.2975/30.4.2007.315.317

Holmes, C. B., & Howard, M. E. (1980). Recognition of suicide lethality factors by physicians, mental health professionals, ministers, and college students. Journal of Consulting and Clinical Psychology, 48(3), 3n83–387.

Javadi, D., Feldhaus, I., Mancuso, A., & Ghaffar, A. (2017). Applying systems thinking to task shifting for mental health using lay providers: a review of the evidence. Global Mental Health, 4, e14., doi.org/10.1017/gmh.2017.15

Matsuzaka, C. T., Wainberg, M., Norcini Pala, A., Hoffmann, E. V., Coimbra, B. M., Braga, R. F., & ... Mello, M. F. (2017). Task shifting interpersonal counseling for depression: A pragmatic randomized controlled trial in primary care. BMC Psychiatry, 17

National Alliance for the Mentally Ill. (2019). Know the warning signs. Retrieved from https://www.nami.org/learn-more/know-the-warning-signs

Payne, J. S., & Hays, K. (2016). A spectrum of belief: A qualitative exploration of candid discussions of clergy on mental health and healing. Mental Health, Religion & Culture, 19(6), 600-612. doi:10.1080/13674676.2016.1221916

Pillion, T., Reed, R., & Shetiman, B. (2012). Mental illness recognition and referral by Catholic priests in North Carolina. Psychiatric Services, 63(5), 510-511. doi:10.1176/appi.ps.20120 p510a

Substance Abuse and Mental Health Services Administration. (2017). National survey on drug use and health. Washington, DC: Author.

Singh, H., Shah, A. A., Gupta, V., Coverdale, J., & Harris, T. B. (2012). The efficacy of mental health outreach programs to religious settings: A systematic review. American Journal Of Psychiatric Rehabilitation, 15(3), 290-298. doi:10.1080/15487768.2012.703557

Su, J., Tsai, C., Hung, T., & Chou, S. (2011). Change in accuracy of recognizing psychiatric disorders by non-psychiatric physicians: Five-year data from a psychiatric consultation–liaison service. Psychiatry and Clinical Neurosciences, 65(7), 618–623.

Svob, C., Wickramaratne, P., Reich, L., Zhao, R., Talati, A., Gameroff, M., Saeed, R., & Weissman, M.(2018). Association of parent and offspring religiosity with offspring suicide ideation and attempts. *JAMA Psychiatry*. doi:10.1001/jamapsychiatry.2018.2060

The United States Conference of Catholic Bishops. (2018). Charter for the protection of children and young people. Washington, DC: Author.

Vermaas, J. D., Green, J., Haley, M., & Haddock, L. (2017). Predicting the mental health literacy of clergy: An informational resource for counselors. Journal Of Mental Health Counseling, 39(3), 225-241. doi:10.17744/mehc.39.3.04

Wang, P. S., Berglund, P. A., & Kessler, R. C. (2003). Patterns and correlates of contacting clergy for mental disorders in the united states. Health Services Research, 38(2), 647–673. http://doi.org/10.1111/1475-6773.00138

Williams, L., Gorman, R., & Hankerson, S. (2014). Implementing a Mental Health Ministry committee in faith-based organizations: The Promoting Emotional Wellness and Spirituality Program. Social Work In Health Care, 53(4), 414-434. doi:10.1080/00981389.2014.880391

APPENDIX A: MINISTRY OPERATIONS

SAMPLE MENTAL HEALTH MINISTRY VOLUNTEER ORIENTATION OUTLINE

1) Scope of The Ministry
2) Diocese Insurance Coverage
3) Training Components
    a) Mental Health First Aid
        i) Verification of training
    b) Making appropriate referrals to vetted mental health providers
4) Job Description
    a) Registered parishioner
    b) Commissioned team members
    c) Auxiliary members
    d) Roles and Guide for serving
5) Confidentiality (not mandated reporters)
6) Monthly Meetings
7) Resources to Know
    a) Community agencies and organizations
    b) Professionals and providers

        c) Referral sites
        d) Monthly tabling
8) Educational Workshops, Training, Presentations, Special Events
        a) Hold at Parishes
        b) Around the Diocese
        c) Community Agency Sponsored Events
9) Data for Mental Health Ministry
        a) How do you know its working?
            i) Annual reports
            ii) Surveys

Sample Description of Roles, Responsibilities and General Guide for Serving

(Support Materials for Volunteers)

While there are descriptive roles and responsibilities for each member, there are no bold dividing lines. The parishioner or family requesting assistance or referred to the ministry is not only the responsibility of one person, or one group, but the whole MInistry.

Ministry Involvement

Team members are expected to attend scheduled meetings and required educational program. The Ministry understands personal and family responsibilities that may conflict with the Mental Health Ministry schedule. It is helpful, that known absence is shared with the Mental Health Ministry Coordinators in advance so that members can plan accordingly.

All members have God-given talents, and some have more time than others, please share them as much as you can.

Communication

Members are expected to read emails and are asked to acknowledge receipt, especially when help is needed for some tasks or projects. If not available or unable to help, please say so in a timely manner, so team can plan accordingly.

Confidentiality

It is expected that all ministry members observe strict confidentiality, and discusses Mental Health Ministry issues formally in private at all times. Sending emails from a personal, non-HIPPA compliant account with individuals' and families' personal information and assistance requests is prohibited.

Sample Mental Health Ministry Planning Calendar

MONTH	ACTIVITY
JANUARY	• Ministry General Meeting • Mental Health Ministry Resource Table • St. Dymphna Prayer Group
FEBRUARY	• Mental Health Ministry Resource Table • Ministry General Meeting • Food for Families • St. John of God Prayer Group
MARCH	• Mental Health Ministry Resource Table • Ministry General Meeting • NAMI speaker • Our Lady of Lourdes Prayer Group
APRIL	• Mental Health Ministry Resource Table • Ministry General Meeting • Educational Event/speaker • St. Benedict Joseph Labre Prayer Group
MAY	• Mental Health Ministry Resource Table • Ministry General Meeting • Community Event • St. Dymphna Prayer Group/Feast Day May 15
JUNE	• Mental Health Ministry Resource Table • Ministry General Meeting • Outreach • St. John of God Prayer Group

JULY	• Mental Health Ministry Resource Table • Ministry General Meeting • Community Event • Our Lady of Lourdes Prayer Group
AUGUST	• Mental Health Ministry Resource Table • Ministry General Meeting • "Conversations Over Breakfast" • St. Benedict Joseph Labre Prayer Group
SEPTEMBER	• Mental Health Ministry Resource Table (Check your Mood screening) • Ministry General Meeting • Educational Event • St. Dymphna Prayer Group
OCTOBER	• Mental Health Ministry Resource Table • Ministry General Meeting • Community Outreach • Educational Event
NOVEMBER	• Mental Health Ministry Resource Table • Ministry General Meeting • Educationally event • St. John of God Prayer Group
DECEMBER	• Mental Health Ministry Resource Table • Ministry General Meeting • Outreach • Our Lady of Lourdes Prayer Group

Sample Mental Health Ministry Bulletin Announcement

Mental Health Ministry

Our parish is a member of the Diocesan Mental Health Ministry Network whose mission is to bring Christ to families experiencing mental health challenges. Individual mental health ministry team members are available to meet and confidentially talk with individuals and families needing support. Ministry members are familiar with the many public and private support services available to families in their local communities and will help families locate suitable providers. Our mental health ministry exists to serve individuals and families experiencing mental illness by offering God's hope and love through encouragement, practical support, and prayer.

If you or a family member are experiencing mental health challenges, please contact a Parish Mental Health Ministry member. You may also contact the Crisis Line (*number in your area)* 24 hours a day/7 days a week.

Appendix B: Sample Prayers

Saint Dymphna, Patron for Those With Mental Illness

Lord we Pray for those who have a Mental Illness

Help us understand that the way we talk about people with a mental illness affects the people themselves and how we treat the illness. So often people who have a mental illness are known as their illness; people say that "she is bipolar" or "he is schizophrenic"; when we talk about mental illness we should not use that phrase. People who have cancer are not cancer; those with heart disease are not heart disease. Let us always remember that people with a mental illness are not the illness – they are beautiful creations of God.

There is so much fear, ignorance and hurtful attitudes that the people who suffer from mental illness needlessly suffer further. Help us to support and be compassionate to those with a mental illness, every bit as much as we support those who suffer from any other illness.

Grant courage to those for whom we pray and fill them with hope. If it is according to Your Divine Will, grant them the recovery and cure they desire. Help them to remember You love them; they are never alone.

Saint Dymphna, Patron of those with a Mental Illness, pray for us.

Prayer to Saint John of God

St. John of God,

patron of the sick and compassionate Brother

to all who suffer or are troubled in any way,

I turn to you with great confidence in my time of need.

I ask you John to speak to Jesus on my behalf.

He will listen to you because you tried to be like Him

in the compassion and love you had for people in need.

I know only Jesus can really help me,

but I also know that He can be influenced by someone close to Him,

I plead with you Brother John

to present this special intention of mine to Jesus

so that He may grant it, according to His will ......(mention the intention).

Help me John to strengthen my faith, my hope and love

for Jesus and our Mother Mary

for whom you had such a special love.

All glory to the Father, Son and the Holy Spirit.

Amen.

PRAYER TO SAINT BENEDICT JOSEPH LABRE

St. Benedict Joseph Labre, you gave up honor, money and home for love of Jesus. Help us to set our hearts on Jesus and not on the things of this world. You lived in obscurity among the poor in the streets. Enable us to see Jesus in our poor brothers and sisters and not judge by appearances. Make us realize that in helping them we are helping Jesus. Show us how to befriend them and not pass them by. St. Benedict Joseph Labre, you had a great love for prayer. Obtain for us the grace of persevering prayer, especially adoration of Jesus in the Most Blessed Sacrament. St. Benedict Joseph Labre, poor in the eyes of men but rich in the eyes of God, pray for us. Amen.

PRAYER FOR THOSE WITH MENTAL ILLNESS

Lord, we pray for those who have a mental illness and those who love and care for them.

So often people who have a mental illness are known as their illness. People say that "she is bipolar" or "he is schizophrenic." When we talk about people who have a mental illness, we should not use that phrase. People who have cancer are not cancer; those with diabetes are not diabetes. People with a mental illness are not illness - they are beautiful creations of God.

The way we talk about people and their illnesses affects the people themselves and how we treat the illness. In the case of mental illness there is so much fear, ignorance and hurtful attitudes that the people who suffer from mental illness needlessly suffer further.

Our society does not provide the resources that are needed to adequately understand and treat mental illness. Even with the best medical care available, always taking the cocktail of medicines that are prescribed and doing their best to be healthy and manage this illness - for too many - that is not enough. Someday a cure will be found, but until then, we need to support and be compassionate to those with mental illness, every bit as much as we support those who suffer from cancer, heart disease or any other illness.

All too often our loved ones who had a mental illness died from suicide. They were sweet, wonderful people who loved life, the people around them- and had faith in you. Eternal rest grant unto them O Lord and may perpetual light shine upon them.

Amen.

Prayer of Petition for Those with a Mental Illness

We remember and pray for those who have a mental illness and those who love and care for them.

The way we talk about people and their illnesses affects the people themselves and how we treat the illness. In the case of mental illness there is so much fear, ignorance and hurtful attitudes that the people who suffer from mental illness needlessly suffer further. We ask God that the fear be turned to love, the ignorance be turned to wisdom and the hurtful attitudes be turned to compassion – we pray to the Lord: **"Lord hear our prayer".**

So often people who have a mental illness are known as their illness; People say that "she is bipolar" or "he is schizophrenic". When we talk about people who have a mental illness we should not use that phrase. People who have cancer are not cancer; those with diabetes are not diabetes. People with a mental illness are not the illness – they are beautiful creations of God. We ask God to help everyone to see them for their goodness, their strength and their beauty – we pray to the Lord: **"Lord hear our prayer".**

Everyone who has a mental illness has a right to the best therapy and medical care available. We ask God that those with a mental illness be encouraged and supported in their efforts to be healthy and manage their illness - we pray to the Lord: **"Lord hear our prayer".**

All too often the medical care that is available is not enough and far too many people suffer. Our society does not provide the resources that are needed to adequately understand and treat mental illness. We ask God to change our society and to give wisdom to our leaders so that every single person suffering from mental illness will receive all the care they need – we pray to the Lord: **"Lord hear our prayer".**

We believe that someday – someday - cures will be found, but until then, we ask God to help us support and be compassionate to those with mental illness, every bit as much as we support those who suffer from cancer, heart disease or any other illness – we pray to the Lord: **"Lord hear our prayer".**

All too often our loved ones who had a mental illness died from suicide. They were sweet, wonderful people who loved life, the people around them- and had faith in you. Eternal rest grant unto them O Lord and may perpetual light shine upon them – we pray to the Lord: **"Lord hear our prayer".**

ABOUT THE AUTHORS

Wendell J. Callahan holds a PhD in Clinical Psychology from the University of California, San Diego and San Diego State University with a specialty in Experimental Psychopathology. Dr. Callahan is a counselor educator and Professor of Practice in the Department of Counseling and Marital & Family Therapy at the University of San Diego, where he is also the Executive Director of the Catholic Institute for Mental Health Ministry. Dr. Callahan is an active member of the St. Brigid Parish Mental Health Ministry in Pacific Beach, CA. Dr. Callahan, his wife and three children are longtime members of the parish.

Liberty Hebron holds a Master of Arts degree in Clinical Mental Health Counseling from the University of San Diego and is a California Licensed Professional Clinical Counselor. Ms. Hebron is also a mental health ministry consultant to the University of San Diego Catholic Institute for Mental Health Ministry, and an adjunct faculty member in the Department of Counseling and Marital & Family Therapy. Ms. Hebron has experience in campus ministry and mental health counseling for incarcerated and families.

Alissa N. Willmerdinger holds a Master of Arts degree in Clinical Mental Health Counseling from the University of San Diego and is a North Carolina Licensed Professional Clinical

Counselor Associate (LPCA). Ms. Willmerdinger completed a research assistantship during her studies at the University of San Diego with the Catholic Institute for Mental Health Ministry. She is currently working as a therapist in a community mental health clinic.